RANCHO DELUXE

RANCHO DELUXE

o o o o o o

Rustic Dreams and Real Western Living

text by ALAN HESS   *photographs by* ALAN WEINTRAUB

CHRONICLE BOOKS

SAN FRANCISCO

ABOVE: *Gordon Lillie turned himself into Pawnee Bill, a leather-fringed impresario whose career stretched from Buffalo Bill's Wild West Show to the movies. His private life underwent an equally radical change: On his Oklahoma ranch he lived in a dirt-floored prairie log cabin until he built his family a magnificent mansion.*

To Maxine, Michael, and Peter Ollove. —A. W.

To Marie Wootten, native of Wyoming's Wind River Canyon and a pioneer in every way. —A. H.

Text © 2000 Alan Hess.

Photography © 2000 Alan Weintraub.

Printed in Hong Kong

Library of Congress Cataloging-in-Publication Data:

Hess, Alan
    Rancho deluxe/Alan Hess, Alan Weintraub.
    p. ; cm.
    Includes bibliographical references and index.
    ISBN 0-8118-2420-9 (hardcover)
    1. Ranch houses—West (U.S.). 2. Interior decorations—West (U.S.).
    I. Weintraub, Alan. II. Title.
    NA7224H47   2000
    728.373   99–29953
    CIP

Cover & interior design: Philip Krayna Design, San Francisco

Cover photograph: Alan Weintraub
Page 2: Pahaska Teepee, the Buffalo Bill Lodge

Distributed in Canada by Raincoast Books
8680 Cambie Street, Vancouver BC V6P 6M9

10 9 8 7 6 5 4 3 2 1

Chronicle Books
85 Second Street, San Francisco, CA 94105
www.chroniclebooks.com

CONTENTS

CHAPTER 2

Deluxe Ranchos : 85

THE OLD WEST AND ITS PRAIRIE DREAMS

THIS is a book about the All-American ranch house. John Wayne's ranch is not in here.

John Wayne never owned a ranch. In 1953 Wayne and his new wife, Pilar, moved into a two-story Early American home on a knoll in Encino. It had five acres, stables, and a riding ring, but no horses.

"Are we going to have horses?" Pilar asked, as she reported in her autobiography.

"Where'd you get that idea?" countered the world's foremost movie cowboy.

"From all your westerns. I just assumed you loved to ride."

"The only time I get on a horse," the Duke replied, "is when I make a movie. I hate the damn things."

That, in a nutshell, is the story of the American ranch house. The image of the ranch house overtook the reality long ago. The ranch was once a practical, dusty, unglamorous homestead, a place of hard work and scant leisure.

But by the middle of the twentieth century the plain, hard-working ranch house of 100 years before had been turned on its head, repackaged as a symbol of relaxation and ease.

It's not often that we get an opportunity to watch a myth develop before our eyes. At this late date we can't know exactly what refinements and alterations tranformed actual experiences into the epics of Homer or the romance of Camelot. But within the memory of our grandparents and greatgrandparents lived the events that

OPPOSITE: *Las Escarbadas (c. 1886). Once headquarters for a division of the three-million-acre XIT Ranch, this building is now preserved at the Ranching Heritage Center at Texas Tech University in Lubbock, Texas.*

turned the ranch into one of America's greatest myths and most enduring architectural styles.

Why does the ranch still have a hold over American architecture? Because of the magic of the movies. The ranch house as we know it today in Ralph Lauren ads and special issues of *Architectural Digest* is a product of the entertainment industry. Building on the tradition of the Wild West shows, movie and television westerns took a rugged, painful, and austere way of life and turned it into a life of romance, adventure, and true grit. They changed a decidedly unromantic and often squalid existence into a shining symbol of individuality, resourcefulness, and contentment.

As much as the sixshooter and the horse, the ranch house became an emblem of that idealized life. Whether it was an adobe house from *El Dorado* or a log cabin from television's *Bonanza*, the lone homestead, a bastion against a forbidding landscape of awesome mountains or desert, held a warm hearth and an indomitable community. The ranch house's hand-hewn timber beams communicated self-reliance, simplicity, and lack of pretensions.

Hollywood gave the ranch a story to tell. By spreading that story for decades, the movies cemented the symbiotic relation between the Western myth and architecture that began with the adoption of a romanticized cowboy style by wealthy Westerners in the early years of the century. In the ranch style, the wood rafters and plank floors put you immediately into a specific place, time, and mood, an atmosphere that recalls not the formalities and class distinctions of Colonial houses but the casual, vernacular, easygoing architecture of log cabins, sod houses, and adobe haciendas. The ranch is an informal, hospitable place, a place to track in dirt and put your boots up. It is peopled with heroes and adventurers, people fighting for justice and helping their neighbors. That's an appealing story.

It's also a story that took time to develop, and that took the ranch house a very long way from its origins as a humble homestead on the prairie. Today the image of the ranch is even more solidly entrenched in the popular imagination than it was in the days of the Old West. Western wear, Western styles, Western art are the subject of magazines, videos, and music, and have stoked the mass migration to the once-empty quarters of Utah, Colorado, Arizona, and Idaho. The sagebrush rebellion reshapes the political landscape. The Old West is even more alive today than it was in the nineteenth century. Suburban housing tracts are filled with split-levels, ramblers, and mini-haciendas that echo the adobe and wood ranchos of the nineteenth century. In the Southwest, the suburban Spanish hacienda style, with its rippling tiled roof, carries on the tradition of the rugged range house gone domestic. In function, purpose, and setting, today's suburban homes have little in common with the isolated, self-sufficient frontier ranch. But the ranch house is one of the great American architectural inventions, a form with the flexibility to adapt and the persistence to remember its roots, even if in the most tenuous ways.

The ranches selected for this volume show a range of styles of ranch house architecture from around the West over the past 150 years. They show how the style evolved from the simple, functional architecture of the nineteenth century to an opulent, vivid style that remains popular today. We include authentic working ranches; the country estates of the Western wealthy, where rustic cowboy architecture was turned into luxury; the homes of media cowboys who helped spread the style to a mass audience as a legend and icon; and finally contemporary examples in suburbia. Together they show how this uniquely American style remained alive by constantly changing.

○   ○   ○

WE BEGIN WITH a look at real ranches. The ranch started out as a utilitarian dwelling and workplace. The ranch house was a place to sleep after exhausting days on the range tending cattle, to eat a solid meal at noon, to keep warm at night. The stables and barns sheltered livestock and hay. Tack rooms, corrals, smokehouses, cisterns, and windmills all were functional structures designed to serve the needs of the cowboys as they went about their business.

Ranch structures and materials varied by location and geography. Usually ranchers used whatever was nearest and cheapest. The yellow stone of northeast Oklahoma gives the ranch house a golden glow; the adobe mud of southern California and New Mexico softens its forms; the forests of Wyoming make wood a favored material there. The ranchers themselves were a source of variety, too. German immigrants to Texas brought different approaches to building than did Spanish immigrants to California. Of course, climate played a part as well; desert climes promoted the use of adobe for cooling and heating, while the snows of Wyoming required sturdy roofs.

Ranches were, in effect, nineteenth-century factories. No less than the shoe factories and textile mills of New England, ranches were spaces organized to produce a product and a profit. They may have been set in exquisite locations—on the Oklahoma prairie, in the mountain meadows of Wyoming, along scenic California coastlines.

But they were factories nonetheless, taking raw grass and animal flesh and turning them into goods and profits.

How did the ranch move from these austere origins to the lush romance of the mythic ranch? Why can every American—and many an Asian and European as well—call up in the mind's eye an image of a ranch? From where did that ubiquitous image come of the simple shack, smoke curling from its chimney, almost lost in a landscape of profound and terrifying majesty?

○   ○   ○

THE ANSWER IS the media.

Before the movies, novels by Ned Buntline, Harvard-educated Owen Wister, and New York dentist Zane Grey were already spreading stories of the West to the mass culture. William Gordon Lillie, born in Illinois in 1860, grew up reading dime novels about the fictitious exploits of his Wild West hero, Buffalo Bill. Lillie actually worked on ranches and lived for a while on a Pawnee reservation, but he was also living at the time that the Wild West was becoming a myth. As Pawnee Bill—sporting a drooping mustache, Stetson hat, and beaded buckskin jacket—he worked for Buffalo Bill's Wild West Show before operating his own show for nearly thirty years. He would ride this horse for the rest of his life.

The upcoming century would be captivated by mass entertainment; even as the ranching West was still thriving, it was being turned into fodder for the myth. Buffalo Bill had been a scout and purveyor of buffalo meat for the crews constructing the railroads. The Miller Brothers, operators of the popular 101 Ranch Wild West Show, ran a highly successful ranch in Osage County, Oklahoma. There was a grain of truth in the claims of men like these to authenticity. But they were also modern men. As the nineteenth century turned to the twentieth, American society was beginning to shift from agriculture to factories, from rural life to cities, from self-sufficient domestic economies to mass consumerism, from hard work to leisure time, from manufacturing to entertainment. Mass media, entertainment, and the public's craving for the exotic—especially at a safe distance—transformed the ranch and the Western lifestyle.

The conceit of the Wild West shows was that the visitors in the stands were witnessing an actual plains encampment from some time in the recent past. Whether its tents and U-shaped ring were set up in Minnesota or New York City or London, visitors were transported to a telescopic view of the Wild West by troupes of more than 200 people. The spectacle, violence, wildlife, and daredevil skills of the Old West were put on display to amaze and entertain a city and small-town audience. Cavalry fought Indians, plainsmen hunted bison, sharpshooters like Annie Oakley displayed extraordinary aiming skills. A way of life spread out over thousands of square miles of land, several states, and scores of years was refashioned, edited, and encompassed in a few hours in a controlled site as a story of adventure, daring, and conquest. This was, of course, a highly edited view of the Western experience, but it helped to shape the consciousness of the American public.

It was a surreal time. Reality turned into show business. Geronimo appeared in the Miller Brothers' 101 Ranch Show wearing a top hat and driving an open touring car. Mae Lillie, a refined Smith graduate, became a sharpshooter in her husband's Wild West show. Later she and her husband adopted an abandoned child who was

rounded up from the streets of Chicago and sent on an orphan train to Oklahoma, there to live in the Lillies' luxurious mansion in the middle of nowhere. In Wyoming, English aristocrats hunted bear with Buffalo Bill Cody. Navajos in Arizona traded for red dye imported from Pennsylvania to perfect their woven rugs. The West may have been exotic, but it was far from isolated.

The culture of entertainment took on a life of its own promoting the Wild West. Soon the baton would be passed to a new generation of myth makers whose medium was the movies. Pioneer Western showman Buffalo Bill made his last show business appearance in 1917 for the 101 Ranch Show. In the same show several stars who would make their mark in movie westerns made their show-business debuts: Buck Jones, Hoot Gibson, Tom Mix, Will Rogers. Mix was a dude wrangler; Rogers performed the rope tricks that would take him to Broadway with Florenz Ziegfeld.

From the Wild West shows it was an easy step to the startling new entertainment technology of the movies. Pawnee Bill had his own movie company on his ranch. So did the Miller Brothers, who wintered their show in 1911 in California, where they formed the 101 Bison Film Company with producer William Ince. As early as 1909, Colonel William Selig brought his film company to the 101 Ranch to film, as did the Pathé Studios.

A modern myth was launched.

o   o   o

THE EXACT APPEARANCE of a romanticized ranch house to fit this myth was not yet formulated. Authentic ranch houses had come in a variety of styles, from the simple, foursquare design of the adobe house on the Chase Ranch in Cimarron, New Mexico, to the linear, Shaker-like simplicity of the Harrell house in Snyder, Texas, to the classic hacienda design of Rancho Camulos in Ventura County, California. A new generation of innovators similarly followed a variety of inspirations. Charles Fletcher Lummis, a star of the newspaper world after he walked across America (actually from Chillicothe, Ohio, to Los Angeles) in 1885, began building himself a river stone hacienda with patios in 1898. Pawnee Bill built a prairie mansion in the Eastern style fitted with dark wood paneling and Renaissance tapestries. Jack London, another media superstar, lived in a modest wood ranch house while he worked on building himself an elaborate mansion, all the while experimenting in progressive farming techniques.

As the West developed its own plutocrats, they required country estates just like their Eastern and European counterparts. Their sources of wealth often were the newly discovered or invented Western assets that became the foundation of the twentieth-century economy: media, oil, mass merchandising. William Randolph Hearst owned a communications empire of newspapers, magazines, and a movie studio; King Gillette invented a cheap, simple, and highly profitable mass market product, the safety razor; Frank Phillips and Edward Doheny ran oil companies.

In the East the wealthy usually built neo-Renaissance cottages at Newport, Rhode Island, or along the Hudson River. The new Western magnates chose to build ranches based on the common vernacular of the West, but of course they managed to scale up the ranch's rough-and-tumble rusticity. Well-known architects helped them to create these "down home" mansions and develop the high-style ranch. Doheny built Ferndale, an adobe-style ranch house designed by Los Angeles architect Wallace

Neff, for a ranch near Santa Paula. Phillips built a replica of the simple Nebraska log cabin he was born in—and then expanded it into a bigger, fancier log cabin. Gillette hired Neff to build an Andalusian farmhouse on a grand scale. And Hearst asked Julia Morgan, still busy designing La Casa Encantada at San Simeon on the coast, to build an inland ranch headquarters near Mission San Antonio de Padua. The old mission of 1771 became the template for the more expansive ranch on a nearby hill. Addison Mizner, image-maker extraordinaire of Palm Beach and Pebble Beach, designed a Spanish-style ranch for the Bradley family outside Colorado Springs.

The Bixby family of Los Angeles had a certifiable link to the early days of ranching in California; George Bixby had bought a Spanish land grant in 1860, including an adobe rancho structure. He lived in it and used it as his headquarters for his 27,000-acre cattle ranch west of the Los Angeles River. Later generations of the family abandoned the old adobe, leaving it to tenants. By the early 1900s it had deteriorated and pigs rambled through its eroding walls. But Llewellyn Bixby remodeled his ancestor's home in 1930, turning it into a rancho deluxe.

In the process he made several changes influenced more by the romantic imagery of old Spanish California featured in the movies than by the stark truth. Instead of restoring the Spanish-era flat roof, or even his ancestor's gabled New England shingled roof, he added a picturesque red tile roof, like those favored in newly reconstructed and stylish Santa Barbara, and turned the tenant farmer's hovel into a luxurious home on a golf course. The rancho had come a long way from its humble beginnings.

These nouveau ranchos allowed their owners to don the mantle of the cowboy. Despite being the head of a major corporation, Frank Phillips had a lifelong fascination with outlaws and hired train robbers and other outlaws to work for him. Guests to Woolaroc sometimes involuntarily participated in faux stagecoach robberies as they were driven in from the Bartlesville train station or airport. On occasion Phillips even allowed a favored guest to shoot one of his ranch's bison.

As these fantasy ranches were being built, the romanticized image that Americans were developing of the West began to twist back on itself. Even as the first cowboy movie stars were gaining a foothold and William S. Hart and Will Rogers were building themselves comfortable ranch mansions, the life of the real ranchers and cowboys—the men and women who got up before dawn to tend cattle and mend fences—continued, as austere and rugged as ever, in contemporary working ranches of the 1920s like the Chapman Barnard Ranch in Pawhuska, Oklahoma. With concrete floors, monkish rooms, and $40 a month pay, the Chapman Barnard had little in common with the Phillips or Doheny ranches or the palatial homes of the movie stars. The working ranches and the myth ranches fostered by the movies existed in strange parallel universes. In the end, the looking-glass ranches became more real to the general public than the originals.

This parallel existence fostered some bizarre excursions from one universe to another. Dude ranches blossomed in the 1930s to allow city folk to vacation in the Wild West, by then as much a state of mind as a geographical location. Average vacationers could ride horses, eat under the stars, and revel in the scenery. The cinematic experience of adventure and pleasure was reflected back onto the real landscape; the architecture of the West began to reflect the celluloid image of it. Tourism, partic-

ularly of the West's natural features, boomed. In an early version of the theme parks that would play such a large role in tourism later in the century, dude ranches provided a quasi-authentic historical and cultural experience for the average American. Dude ranches like the Kenyon Ranch in Tubac, Arizona, and the Kemper Campbell Ranch in Victorville, California, proved that the ranch had a new life in the new Western economy of travel, entertainment, and recreated experience.

If it had not been for their new role, and their glorification in the movies, ranches might well have disappeared from the landscape. Instead the ranch adapted and survived, albeit in altered form, and remained a living part of the culture. The outer world shapes our inner dreams; in turn, they can shape the world outside. Hollywood's dreamlike re-creation of the West reached out to redesign the real world in its own image.

Gene Autry, Roy Rogers, Hopalong Cassidy, Montie Montana, and Leo Carrillo rarely ventured near a photographer without their sombrero or ten-gallon hat, bandanna, Western shirt with piping and bucking-bronco stitchery, and boots. In the public eye, their homes, like their costumes, were an extension of their screen roles; you can't imagine any of them living in a New York brownstone.

Their ranches were on the whole neater, more glamorous, and more prosperous than most of the ranches that appeared in their movies. Will Rogers' Pacific Palisades ranch was half ranch, half Beverly Hills mansion. Art directors like Hal Pereira, Carl Anderson, Lyle Wheeler, Russell Kimball, James Basevi, Alfred Ybarra, and others usually dressed their movie western sets with an authentic sense of clutter and grime. Fast-forward through the scenes depicting ranches in westerns: the cattle baron's ranch in John Wayne's *McClintock*, the adobe ranch house in Gene Autry's *In Old Santa Fe*, the wood porch in *The Searchers*. Here ranches are the embodiment of rugged individualism, shelters for pioneers eking out a living despite harsh nature and wicked people. Bravery, justice, hard work, and even the tragedy of fate suffuse the sets; so do family ties and loyalty. The cowboy stars' homes were meant to express the same values, but in idealized form.

It was in these movie star houses of the 1920s and 1930s that the cowboy style was codified. These homes exhibited, in a remarkably consistent manner, the all-embracing nature of the Western style. Will Rogers' living room, from the rough-hewn log trusses to the lovingly carved horsehead beam supports to the staunchly upright dining chairs, shows the aesthetic consistency of the cowboy style. The materials are natural; the craftsmanship is by hand, a popular version of the Craftsman aesthetic itself; the form is simplicity itself. Pretension, fanciness, and classical precedent and ornament are excluded. With its Navajo blankets, lariats, saddles, and other talismans of the West, Rogers' house was a shrine to vanished ways of life.

There is a self-referential quality to these cowboy designs. They embraced a pan-Westernism, no matter where they were located. Pawnee Bill's living room is decorated with paintings of Western mountains and cowboys—scenes that are far from the rolling grassland of Oklahoma, where the ranch is situated. Not far away the dining room of the Cross Bell Ranch—a real but modernized working ranch—is encircled by a 1943 incised linoleum mural of a cowboy roundup. It tells an engaging story of stately Indians and of happy cowboys roping calves or chowing down at the chuck wagon while hopping jackrabbits and wily coyotes provide comic relief—all set in the craggy buttes and dry ground of Arizona, say, or southern Texas. The Monument Valley scenes of John Ford westerns have so infused the popular imagination's sense of the West that even among ranchers the cowboy scenes of the movies are the defining image.

So it is that even real ranches have come to reflect their celluloid image. But in an up-and-down industry that cannot be logically justified simply on the basis of profits, ranchers do speak of a love of their craft and lifestyle. These artifacts and reminders on the walls seem to represent the deeper appeal of ranching that keeps them at it—at least until they go broke for the last time.

In part the cowboy star homes that codified the Western style were a public relations strategy. But even more they show the power and appeal of storytelling in the movies. The stars wanted to be part of the story told in westerns in their real life; the public wanted to be part of the story, too. Living in ranch houses was one way to live out the dream.

In these idealized ranches, the visual essence of the West was concentrated, organized, and harmonized. No actual ranch of the last century was as thoroughly and lavishly styled as these homesteads. Individual artifacts may be traceable to authentic sources: oil lanterns did hang from ceilings historically; mounted steer horns were placed over doors and fireplaces. But time, expense, and lack of opportunity made such intensely conceived scenes as the Rogers ranch unlikely in the real West.

But that is what makes the stars' homes significant. Here is an authentic American style, based on native materials and vernacular forms, raised to the sumptuousness and clarity of any other style, Colonial, Gothic, or

Modern. The raw data of the ranch vernacular has been reworked, edited, abstracted, compressed, and turned into a flexible architectural vocabulary. The cowboy style is not simply a historical re-creation; it is a great work of the imagination.

○   ○   ○

IN MOST GENE AUTRY movies there comes a scene in which Gene, riding his horse, Champion, is chasing and shooting at bad guys who are riding in something like black 1940 Buick convertibles. The scene is emblematic of the timelessness of the cowboy style. Ever since the movies, it has existed out of time and space. Those serials brought the Old West of cowboys and bad guys to the real 1940s. No explanation or excuse was offered. History and fantasy overlap.

The Old West continues to live as an image as strongly as ever. From Rancho Camulos to Pawnee Bill's prairie mansion to Frank Phillips' Woolaroc to the latest Ralph Lauren advertisement, the ranch style has constantly adapted to the times yet remained recognizable. There is no pure ranch style; it is constantly reinterpreted. Yet it always retains a cohesion of meaning and look. Contradictions don't matter. Movie cowboy William S. Hart was born in New York. One of the first westerns, *The Great Train Robbery*, was filmed in New Jersey. Ranch style is the product of a constant dialectic of East and West, mongrel, perhaps, but obviously vital.

This vitality and timelessness helped the ranch style make the crossover to the suburbs after 1945. The ranch house and suburbia have a long-standing, symbiotic relationship. The ranch house offered the perfect image and architecture for the suburban tracts opening after World War II. Even the original Levittown, in the heart of Long Island, had so-called ranch models—basically New England salt boxes, but built close enough to the ground and with barely enough decorative features to qualify as ranches. Levitt's appropriation of the ranch image showed its usefulness in marketing across the nation. The idea of a ranch included the wide-open prairies, an appealingly anti-urban selling point for buyers moving out of the crowded cities. The distance between the reality of the stilted Levittown ranch and the image ranch as the movies portrayed it made little difference.

For such a traditional style—wagon-wheel chandeliers, board-and-batten walls, shake roofs, stone fireplaces—the ease with which it could be altered and redefined is astonishing. This adaptability is also probably what keeps it a living style. No one was more influential in balancing this Western tradition and innovation than southern California architect Cliff May, with the aid of *Sunset Magazine* ("The Magazine of Western Living"). May was one of several Western architects fascinated with the haciendas and ranch houses, both working establishments and those in ruins, around the West in the 1920s and 1930s. He wrote a paean to the ranch in 1946 that included many of his home designs—designs that he presented as ranch style, but that in reality were a radical reinterpretation of the style. Authentic ranches were pragmatic; May's ranch houses were romantic. They gloried in their natural settings and faced the views; indeed, they brought the scenic outdoors inside through large, modern sliding doors and plate-glass windows. Doors and porches made the inside and outside easily accessible to each other, as in traditional ranches, but for the mid-twentieth-century lifestyle the real purpose was to make the pool and garden easier to reach. Like the ranch homes of the cowboy stars, May's houses picked and chose among the possibilities or spaces, materials, and shapes offered by traditional ranches, and so created a vivid and highly popular architectural style suited to the emerging suburban lifestyle. The low, rambling ranch house with shake roofs and board siding became a staple of suburban tracts.

These suburban homes were an art form in themselves. Whitewashed stucco walls brought back memories of adobe haciendas like the Camulos home in California. Wood-sided ranches with wooden front porches called up the memory of log cabins in Wyoming and Texas. Whether brick, adobe, or wood, the materials spoke of simplicity, of using the material nearest at hand to build a solid shelter in the harsh environment as quickly as possible. The low, rambling profile; the room wings jutting out here and there; the front porch as a sophisticated way to negotiate the social interactions of strangers, guests, and family; the power of the rustic image of rough-hewn wood beams, rough adobe surfaces, and unpainted planks of wood; the tactile appeal of exposed rock—all suited many modern home buyers.

The decorative elements also helped the ranch home tell a story. Wagon-wheel chandeliers were popular in latter-day ranch-style houses because they spoke of the resourcefulness of the owner, ready to use anything at hand to solve a problem. The image became an indispensable feature of the style.

But if in the beginning the suburbs claimed the image of the ranch, today the suburbs are actually claiming the ranches themselves. As ranch and farm land on the edge of metropolitan areas is developed, many ranches have been swallowed by the suburbia their kind helped to popularize. The Chatsworth ranch where Roy Rogers and Dale Evans lived in the 1950s has disappeared into a ranch-style subdivision with streets named Dale Court and Trigger Street at the far western reaches of the San Fernando Valley. Ironically, the nearby movie ranches of Corriganville and Iverson Ranch, where many westerns were filmed amid red rock spires, have also disappeared into the suburban maw. Where a lone ranch house (or set) once stood in this photogenic desert, now hundreds of suburban ranchos clamber up the slopes and sit next to the house-sized boulders.

The ranch house is, then, a true twentieth-century architecture. It is a combination of the motifs of the past with the needs of the present, achieved with new materials but playing on the cultural imagination and memories of the popular audience. By now it has an unbreakable connection with the movies, which gave the ranch meaning and continue to spread its fame. Had that technology not existed, the ranch house would most probably have gone the way of log cabins and sod huts, a colorful historical memory but no longer a living architecture.

Was there ever a "real" West? One thing is certain: by the late twentieth century, the ranch had existed longer as an image in popular culture than it had as a place to work cattle. The country's most famous dude rancher, Theodore Roosevelt, wrote, "The best days of ranching are over . . . The great free ranches, with their barbarous, picturesque and curiously fascinating surroundings . . . must pass away before the onward march of our people." That was written in 1888. The real ranch and its barbarous surroundings may indeed have passed away since then, but the ranch as a myth remains very much alive today.

CHAPTER 1

REAL COWBOYS

WHETHER they are set in the mountains, deserts, or plains of the West, the working ranches and ranch houses of the nineteenth and early twentieth centuries do not always match the image of the romantic ranch of the movies. Most often they are simple, practical buildings fashioned of adobe, brick, or wood and made comfortable with a few ornamental items. Less often, they are large estate houses that use the transplanted styles of the East to temper the West's harsh and isolated life. Yet pick among them and you may find the raw materials that later generations, farther from the rigors of life on the range, came to treasure and elevate into a memorable style to remind them of the West, wherever they were.

LEFT: *Chase Ranch, New Mexico. Family mementos surround the cherry-wood bedstead in the spacious master bedroom. The Victorian-era bed, a symbol of the civilizing influence of ranchers like the Chases, was brought from St. Louis by oxcart.*

ABOVE: *Palm trees and lawn now landscape the Rancho Camulos courtyard. In 1848 it would have been both dustier and busier. Cooks, children, rancheros, and vaqueros used this area, in front of the separate kitchen wing, as a scullery, playroom, and lounge. The shingles, newly replaced, are typical of roof coverings in the period, when the roof was not flat.*

OPPOSITE: *Until recently, Ranch Camulos was a working ranch headquarters. Now undergoing restoration, it will become a part of the Ventura County Museum of History and Art as a showplace of early California life.*

RANCHO CAMULOS
VENTURA COUNTY, CALIFORNIA, 1848

Ghosts walk at Rancho Camulos. There are the quiet ghosts of vaqueros and cooks, rancheros and children who worked or played in the dusty court 150 years ago. But there are other, noisier ghosts that still haunt the national imagination, like the ghost of Helen Hunt Jackson. An Easterner who became one of the first and most effective mythologizers of rancho life and architecture, Jackson lived at Rancho Camulos for a time. Her innocent visit links the ranch to two worlds: the reality of life on authentic ranchos in the early days of European California, and the approaching glorification of that life in novels, Wild West shows, and movies. She used what she saw of the remainders of hacienda life in writing the novel *Ramona*, which in some ways is the *Uncle Tom's Cabin* of California. The heyday of Spanish-Mexican California was already past, but that made it even easier for her to see in the remains the better world in which the people of the past eternally live. Through her work the real ranch of the past dovetails with the mythic ranch of today.

Now under restoration, Rancho Camulos is a classic hacienda. Three wings frame a broad central court. Today it is filled with a garden of tall palms, brick walks, and lawn. A century ago it was a Victorian garden of small ornamental palms set in a dusty court. In the time of the *Californios,* it was a bare and dusty workplace.

Another ghost at Rancho Camulos is that of architect Cliff May, the popularizer of the suburban ranch house in the 1930s and 1940s. He studied Camulos and other ranchos. May visited the ranch even longer after the heyday of the rancho than Jackson did. The passage of time was an advantage for May, too; the run-down adobe walls lent themselves to suggestive readings. May could see the outlines of the house and its life—the doors that connected every room to the out-of-doors, the shady porches, the way the building followed the gentle slope of the land, the casual ramble of its wings. The building and its U-shaped courtyard had a spare simplicity and yet reflected a communal complexity. Many people lived here; it was home, office, warehouse, chapel, school, playground, fiesta site.

TOP: *The wings of the house rested flat on the gently sloping site, requiring many steps from wing to wing. The teepee fireplace is a later addition.*

LEFT: *Thick walls and heavy plank doors suggest the occasional need for early ranchos to become defensive sanctuaries. Rancho Camulos is still set in a valley floor of citrus groves, a rare example of a landscape within an hour of Los Angeles that has changed little in 200 years.*

OPPOSITE: *The working rancho was a compound of buildings including barns, stables, and bunkhouses, as well as the chapel shown here.*

ABOVE: *Thick adobe walls required heavy buttresses to shore them up. The ground-hugging, U-shaped building with its open court is typical of the Spanish era in California, Arizona, and New Mexico.*

OPPOSITE: *With its southern exposure, this tall porch scooped up the sun and created a pleasant place to sit on a sunny winter morning.*

On a cool but sunny morning a ranchero could sit on the high-ceilinged porch, a sun catcher on the south side of the house. The heat of the day might find him lounging on the shady porch that fronted three sides of the courtyard. It was an informal way of life, startlingly different from the formality implied by an American Colonial house. Each room leads into the next; there are no indoor corridors. Instead the exterior porch, or *corredor*, was the way from room to room in sunshine or rain, day or night. May saw this as a way of life for California. He picked and chose what he liked about the building's features and rearranged them in his designs for the mid-twentieth-century suburban house.

In Rancho Camulos you can see most of the ideas that evolved into the twentieth-century ranch house: the low, casual lines, the simple materials, the indoor spaces connected to the outside, the rooms lined up in a row. But you also see how things change. Some elements have faded away, like the separate kitchen that would be incorporated in the main building in the typical ranch-style house. Other elements take on a new life, like the porches and outdoor spaces, the informal composition of different buildings loosely held together, and the way the placement of doors and windows reflects the interior plan without any concern for a symmetrical, formal facade to impress visitors.

SAN AUGUSTINE RANCH

LAS CRUCES, NEW MEXICO, 1855

Today the sunny courtyard of the San Augustine ranch is a garden, a friendly workplace, a roofless vestibule for greeting visitors. A peach tree sprouted from a long-ago discarded pit adds color and life. The adobe porch's sun screen, a curtain of wood with a Victorian-style, dart-shaped fringe, offers protection from the heat and glare.

The ranch sits beneath the ragged silhouette of the Organ Mountains in the windy wastes of the Tularosa Basin in southern New Mexico, as dry and sublimely desolate a landscape as you'll find out west. This is the West of endless views, of tumbleweeds and ranges of naked rock. The courtyard's big adobe walls and comforting shelter are an oasis out here.

But 120 years ago the same pleasant courtyard had a more serious purpose. It helped to create a fortress against the violence of the time. Then, no door allowed entry to the court; ladders, which could be pulled up in case of attack, were the only way in. Most of the house's exterior walls were windowless, so the court offered the sole access to sun and air. The house's well lay within the courtyard walls. The flat roofs of the adobe house were part of its defenses as well. Made of thick dirt tamped down on chevron-patterned branches resting on thick log vigas, they offered a vantage point for shooting at attacking Apaches.

ABOVE: *A collection of skulls and antlers encrusts the gateposts of the original ranch. The high wall in the distance was originally a practical defense; before the door was added, only ladders allowed entry to the house. Building the gate was one of the typical, peaceful chores of Wain Brazell, a trusted ranch hand who worked for rancher Bill Cox around the turn of the century. Shooting Sheriff Pat Garrett in retaliation for Garrett's killing of another ranch hand was one of his less typical chores.*

OPPOSITE: *The sagebrush of the dry Tularosa Basin and the serrated peaks of the Organ Mountains form a rugged setting for the San Augustine Ranch. Back in the days when the site was a stage stop and hotel, visitors could be seen approaching from miles away.*

ABOVE: *San Augustine has been in the hands of the same family for three generations. Additions and changes have preserved the style of the original. This new screen door copies turn-of-the-century screen doors, but the view over the dry range is original.*

RIGHT: *Native Americans living in the area left behind stone metates, used for grinding meal for their food.*

ABOVE: *The current owner's grandfather added this wooden sunshade, a graceful Victorian touch to an austere, Spanish-era adobe structure.*

RIGHT: *Fruit trees now blossom in the sheltered courtyard, from the beginning a haven from the harsh winds and blistering sun of the southern New Mexico desert.*

The one-time inn and stage stop on the road to the salt mines has mellowed. Run since 1893 by three generations of the Cox family, the gracious house is a mark of a West that always changes but always honors its past. Today an arcaded porch looks east out over the buildings of the White Sands Missile Testing Range in the valley below; in 1946 the government took ninety-one percent of the ranch, which once encompassed 150,000 acres. The first atomic bomb was tested only eighty-five miles to the north in 1945. Ranches can't escape the changing times.

Under the stewardship of Robert and Murnie Cox, the house's history continues. Robert's grandmother's kitchen has become the master bedroom, but still in place is the doorway that Sheriff Pat Garrett kicked down in 1899 as he searched for an Oklahoma murderer. So is the hallway where Garrett shot down the young ranch worker he suspected of being the culprit. The charge was never proven, but Robert Cox will show you the two bullets that were dug out of the adobe walls after the incident. Even the walled courtyard couldn't protect the house from all of the West's violence.

ABOVE: *Chase selected the rolling, piñon-dotted hills of northern New Mexico, near the track of the Santa Fe Trail, as the site of the first of many ranches he had an interest in while helping to settle this once-wild area.*

OPPOSITE: *Unlike the low, U-shaped adobe ranchos built by the Spanish elsewhere in the West, this adobe shows Yankee influences. The two-story center is the core of the house; the dining room wing to the left and the kitchen wing to the right were added later.*

CHASE RANCH

CIMARRON, NEW MEXICO, 1871

Not all adobe ranches in the Southwest are flat-roofed houses arranged around a walled court like the traditional Spanish haciendas of southern California and Santa Fe. Theresa and Manly Chase's earthen homestead was foursquare and compact, with four big rooms and no corridors, inside or out. Even today a porch along the southeast side looks out on the remnants of Manly's apple orchard, his pride and joy.

In 1879, after giving birth to her sixth child, Theresa decided that her growing family needed more room. She built up, piling more adobe blocks atop the existing walls, three bricks wide, and adding a steep staircase to the four new rooms enclosed by the new walls—all in five weeks while her husband was away on a cattle drive. The house is Territorial style, a mix of Spanish adobe and Yankee formality. As the Chases added more rooms—a generous dining room for entertaining thirty guests at a time, a kitchen wing, a bigger and more comfortable master bedroom with tin cove-molding and even a fashionable bay window to catch the sun—they clustered them around the square main house.

The Chases and their ranch house were part of the taming of the West. Built near the Santa Fe Trail, the Chase ranch reflected the trade of ideas and goods along

the main lifeline connecting Hispanic New Mexico with the United States. As Manly and Theresa's family grew and the ranch prospered—and even when it did not, given the uncertain fortunes of ranching—they sent back east for furnishings, drapes, chinaware, and other examples of a refined life to be shipped overland in wagons.

Still in the parlor are the grand piano, the fashionable rocking chairs, the fringed curtains flecked with metallic thread—all a startlingly bold statement of the Chases' faith that the Wild West would not remain wild. Considering the history of the town of Cimarron, that was a brave faith to hold. Bloody wars over land rights broke out regularly in the 1870s. Corrupt Indian agents provoked Indian attacks. The Chases were in the middle of these events, offering their home as a place to negotiate with the Native Americans and gathering respected

TOP: *Although adobe was used for the house, the Chases brought wood from the mountains nearby for their barns and stables.*

LEFT: *Most of the working buildings of the Chase Ranch are log instead of adobe.*

OPPOSITE: *This pedestal-legged grand piano was brought by wagon from the East. The globe shows the Chases' interest in the world outside provincial New Mexico; the family albums on the piano show the ongoing story of the family and the ranch. The quilt was stitched by Aunt Abbie in 1886.*

citizens to protest unfair treatment of the Utes and the Jicarillo Apaches. All the while they bought interests in new ranches and businesses to help settle and stabilize the region. By 1875 Manly was tending 100,000 sheep and 30,000 heads of cattle.

Gretchen Sammis, the Chases' great-granddaughter, runs the ranch today with her forewoman, Ruby Gobble, aided at roundup time by a team of off-duty schoolteachers who double as cowgirls. Gretchen cares for the house as carefully as she cares for the family mementos and furnishings handed down to her. In recent years she has replaced the cedar shingles with a galvanized metal roof and recoated the adobe walls. Unlike the dry desert climate that preserves the adobe bricks of houses like the Kemper Campbell Ranch in Victorville, California, the snow and rain of New Mexico dictate constant care for the house to keep things the way they were.

RIGHT: *The irregular forms and uneven lines of the fireplace mark it as handmade adobe. This small room off the kitchen has served as a bedroom, mudroom, infirmary, and television room in the ever-changing ranch house.*

OPPOSITE: *During the cold months, this room serves as the warm core of the house. The parlor is through the door on the right, the dining room through the door on the left.*

ABOVE: *Whether the ranch was big or small, ranchers on the frontier in the 1870s usually wanted to surround themselves with signs of fine taste from the East Coast, like the silver on this sideboard and the prints on the walls.*

LEFT: *The efficient kitchen boasts everything from built-in flour bins and collections of pewter and copper utensils to the off-kilter angles of adobe walls.*

OPPOSITE: *The Chases' enormous dining room could seat large groups. It was a crucial socializing tool in their push to turn a wild, lawless country into a peaceful ranching community. The built-in cabinets at the far end hold several complete sets of china; one cabinet door is a disguised doorway that leads to a room beyond.*

ABOVE: *Rifles, saddles, helmets, canes, and over a century's worth of collected books form the treasure of this ranch, which has been owned and operated by the same family for four generations.*

LEFT: *The curio cabinet, built into what was once a door from the parlor to the dining room, displays arrowheads, unusual rocks, petrified wood, metates, and other examples of the Chases' interest in their region's rich history.*

OPPOSITE: *The parlor was originally two rooms of the original four-room house. But as the family grew and a second floor was added, a magnificent arch was cut through the adobe to create a spacious parlor. The room features a wide selection of rocking chairs. At Christmas a decorated tree stands under the arch.*

JA RANCH

PALO DURO CANYON, TEXAS, 1875

Even if you're driving a pickup, it's hard to see over the high brush on the flat plains east of Amarillo, Texas. There are no rises. There are no distant landmarks. So it is startling when, without warning, the flat land drops away beneath your feet and Palo Duro Canyon opens up.

The canyon's pink, salmon, and ocher strata are a geological mural of the past, a relic of ancient seas and great upheavals. And in its way the beautifully preserved JA Ranch is a panoramic mural of Texas ranching and some of its most famous names.

There's the original squared-log cabin, about forty by fifteen feet, a rough yet solidly built home. Here was the headquarters for Charles Goodnight, who gave his name to one of the Southwest's most famous cattle trails. With financial backing from Irishman John Adair, Goodnight was able to make a reality of his long-planned ranch in Palo Duro Canyon. After Adair died, his wife, Cornelia, and her children by a previous marriage returned from England to keep hand-son control of the ranch in the family. Cornelia's granddaughter and namesake, Cornelia (Ninia) Bivins, continues the role today.

The ranch prospered early. From stone quarried on the ranch, several buildings were added. A stone bunkhouse built with a broad plank porch and hand-made benches has proven over the years to be just the right place for whiling away leisure hours. Longhorn

ABOVE: *The JA's main house is a mixture of Queen Anne and Craftsman styles, but to the left can be seen the original two-story log cabin, which served as the initial homestead.*

OPPOSITE: *Touches like the wood paneling in the study of the main house may echo owner Cornelia Adair's years in England.*

skulls and oil lamps sit in the windows of the day room, and a deck of cards lies on the floor. The long dining table in the mess hall is the regular center of meals. Eight wood bunks are built into the bunk room.

For its own living quarters the family built a large addition to the old log cabin. Its broad twin dormers and wide porch are a mix of Queen Anne and Craftsman bungalow styles. Inside it is Texas Victorian. Carved wood mantels reach toward the tall ceilings. The study is paneled with formal ornamental molding, but French doors make it easy to step out onto the porch to drink in the expansive view of the canyon.

The house belongs to the period before ranches self-consciously displayed their own rusticity and began to celebrate the symbols of a hard, handmade, ad hoc way of life. Here there are no settees made of hand-hewn branches, no wagon-wheel chandeliers. This ranch house is quite happy with machine-made gingerbread as its symbol of the advance of progress and civilization in the rugged West.

TOP: *Oilcloth covers the mess hall's dining table. Fiberboard ceilings, a steer head, and an antique hutch blend with the ketchup bottles and salt shakers to create a true rough-and-ready style.*

LEFT: *The stone bunkhouse still serves as the working center of the ranch. Here the cowboys come to eat, to lounge on the porch's handmade benches beneath cattle skulls, and to sleep in the wood bunks. The structure also includes apartments for the ranch's families.*

OPPOSITE: *Eight bunk beds were ready for the ranch hands, though in warm weather Texas cowboys often slept outside even when they weren't out on the range.*

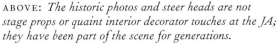

ABOVE: *The historic photos and steer heads are not stage props or quaint interior decorator touches at the JA; they have been part of the scene for generations.*

TOP: *The first floor of the original ranch cabin, now a sitting room, shows the solid logs of the walls inside and out. The stitchery on the couch cushions, depicting saguaro and barrel cactus, reflects the popular image of the West more than the actual scenery around the JA.*

RIGHT: *The ranch office has its own rough, thrown-together style, tempered by refined touches. The maps and rifle are practical; the awards and photos of cattle are clearly a point of pride; and a delicate wallpaper border around the rim of the ceiling shows an aesthetic fastidiousness.*

OPPOSITE: *A bedroom on the second floor of the old log cabin, now a wing of the main house, is reached by a narrow, steep stairway.*

HARRELL RANCH HOUSE

SNYDER, TEXAS, 1883–1917

What is a true ranch house? Is it a one-room stone cabin with a pitched roof? Is it the wood frame structure that was added to that cabin as the family and the ranch grew? Is the real ranch style found in the roughly laid stone of the early days or in the attempts at gracious touches like the gingerbread adorning the porch columns?

A living ranch house changes constantly. At the Harrell Ranch House, each period of the ranch's history has left its trace. Once situated on the V Bar Ranch in Scurry County, the house has been moved to the Ranching Heritage Center at Texas Tech University in Lubbock, a refuge for ranch structures that would otherwise be demolished. Here the Harrell home forms one link in the chain of ranch architecture and ranch life, from dugouts to log cabins to grand prairie mansions.

TOP: *The small, one-room stone cabin was the first prairie home for the Harrell Ranch. The shingle and board shed were added as the family and ranch grew. The Harrell Ranch was moved from its original site and now stands at the Ranching Heritage Center in Lubbock, Texas.*

LEFT: *The classic ranch house was a single-gabled structure with a porch along one side. This wing of the Harrell Ranch House was a later addition to the stone cabin.*

OPPOSITE: *In the kitchen inexpensive, two-inch-wide wood slats, common siding material in the early twentieth century, were used on the walls and ceiling.*

The almost Shaker-like simplicity of ranch architecture was a necessity, not a choice. Any materials that could not be cut or quarried on the ranch required expensive hauling, usually by wagon. Fancy materials or furnishings were a sign of luxury. Simple tongue-and-groove wood strips were commonly used for wainscot, walls, and ceilings.

Unlike California ranches designed on the Spanish model of two or three wings built around a courtyard, many Texas ranches were planned like a train, with a line of rooms one after the other. One room opened into the next. The porches acted as corridors as well as rooms in their own right that provided relief from the heat inside during the summers. The Harrells liked them so much that they built three porches onto their house over the years.

TOP: *Milled wood paneling was added to the inside walls of the original cabin as the one-room house expanded. The room later became a bedroom.*

RIGHT: *Hedwig Hill cabin (c. 1850). This typical dog-trot house—an open-air, covered breezeway cuts between two log cabins—has the simple gable roof, the outdoor porch, and the obvious additions of a traditional ranch that grew as it prospered. Originally from Bexar County, Texas; now at the Ranching Heritage Center.*

OPPOSITE: *The plainest of materials and the simplest of ornament made a ranch a home. There was no effort to bring self-consciously Western elements such as wagon-wheel chandeliers or lariat-styled ornament into these ranch homes; the cowboy style had not yet been codified. That would require the help of Hollywood.*

OW Ranch

DECKER, MONTANA, 1890

John Kendrick brought his bride, Eula, to a log cabin on Montana's Hanging Woman Creek in 1891. He was the ranch's managing superintendent then, but by 1897 he would own the spread. That was just the start of a career based on the Western wealth of ranching, mining, and banking that would lead him to the Wyoming governor's mansion and then to the Capitol in Washington as one of the state's senators.

The upward trajectory of Kendrick's career eventually allowed him to move his family to an opulent home in the Wyoming town of Sheridan, but until then the log cabin on the range was home. The cabin nestled against the hills could be the model for the ranch house as it came to be constructed in the national imagination in future decades. Its rustic walls were fashioned of

OPPOSITE: *The remodeled dining room of the main house uses wood wainscoting and tin ceilings, common manufactured building materials at the turn of the century.*

TOP: *The amenities of ice house, bathhouse, and spring house were added in 1902, when one-time cowboy John Kendrick was becoming a leading citizen of the region. He would eventually serve as Wyoming governor and U.S. senator.*

RIGHT: *The stone buildings behind the main house and bunkhouse accommodated a tall ice house (ice was packed between layers of sawdust), a vaulted spring house for cooling milk, a meat locker, and a bathhouse with a wood stove and a tub.*

squared-off, hand-hewn logs, dovetailed at the corners. A plank porch overlooked the valley. Eula Kendrick filled the whitewashed cabin with $900 worth of furnishings—drapes, lace, oil lamps, wardrobes with beveled glass, and that icon of civilization, a piano—to make it a fit place to raise their two children.

But the ranch still kept the rugged character of the range. A natural spring ran through troughs in the stone spring house to keep milk and perishables cool. The ranch house was shingled, but the bunkhouse, stable, and barns had thick sod roofs. To support the weight, massive pine logs up to eighteen inches thick formed their post and beam structures. These solid frameworks, mellowed golden with age, are a grand memory of the work, sweat, and hopes of Kendrick and other ranchers.

TOP: *Known originally as the White House because it was painted white, the log house of the OW Ranch must have nearly faded into the winter setting.*

LEFT: *The piece-sur-piece construction of the barns was once common in this part of the West; the horizontal logs are shaped to fit into a groove in the intermittent vertical posts.*

OPPOSITE: *The hefty logs of the roof trusses of the stables and bunkhouse originally had to hold up a heavy sod roof—and a layer of snow in winter. They were logged at the Custer National Forest north of here.*

The family left the ranch behind when they moved to a three-story, Flemish-style mansion in Sheridan in 1913. Kendrick named that house Trail End and decorated his son Manville's room with an Indian-pattern stencil, but those were the only nods to the ranching culture the Kendricks had left behind. Unlike Pawnee Bill's prairie mansion of the same period, there were no ceramic tiles of pioneer wagon treks ornamenting the mantelpieces. The new house looked east for inspiration.

Today Kendrick's original ranch is being restored by James Guercio. He's jacking up foundations and replacing termite-riddled wood. The OW is no longer anywhere near the 400,000 acres Kendrick once controlled over his several ranches. But it continues to be a working ranch, largely unmodernized. It is one of the dwindling number of places where the way of life of a hundred years ago continues to work today.

TOP: *A central sitting room leads to a bedroom through the right door and a bathroom (once a bedroom) on the left. Though the furnishings are not original, they are in the style of the ranch's period.*

LEFT: *A latter-day lounge chair incorporates stitchery in a Western theme.*

OPPOSITE: *The strictly Victorian chandelier and screens mix with rugged cowboy elements, like the low coatracks for slickers and saddles brought inside.*

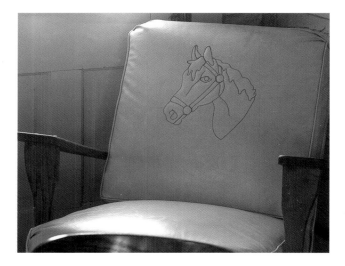

ABOVE: *The interiors today are simpler than when the Kendricks lived here with their two children. Then, as at the JA, the Chase, the Barton, and other well-to-do Victorian-era ranches, the rooms were filled with knick-knacks, carved wood furniture, and framed pictures.*

RIGHT: *Still a working ranch, the OW has also been preserved as an example of Montana life a century ago.*

OPPOSITE: *The remodeled kitchen combines antiques with an 1890s-style wood-burning stove and built-in cabinets in the spirit of the original era.*

BARTON HOUSE

HALE COUNTY, TEXAS, 1909

By 1909 the railroad reached to most places in Texas and the West. It made possible this extraordinary vision: a Victorian-style home sitting by itself in the flat prairie. The materials for the house were shipped by train from a factory to Amarillo, loaded onto wagons, and driven south to a ranch in Hale County. There they were assembled according to the designs in an architectural plan book.

Normally such a house would be seen on a tree-lined street in some American town, flanked by neighbors similar in style and size only several yards away. With its widow's walk and Palladian windows, this house seems out of place all by itself. It stands too tall; its ornament is incongruous in the hot sun and featureless grassland. It is no kin to the stone ranches and one-story ranch houses that were more typical in Texas at the turn of the century.

But the image of a town home was precisely what the owner desired. A house this magnificent displayed confidence. It was a vision of the hoped-for future. It suggested an entire town in itself. The carefully designed proportions of dormers and gables showed that its owner could think about more than crude necessity. The design represented a leap of faith that sometimes paid off and sometimes did not.

Inside, a central hall featured an elaborate, wood-paneled staircase. High ceilings and generous rooms helped to combat the stifling heat of summer, but the wood frame house did not adapt to the hot climate in the way that stone or adobe did, cooling in summer and warming in winter.

That didn't matter. This house was a sign that the West had arrived. People here could live just as well as anyone, anywhere in the nation.

ABOVE: *The varied gables, porches, and loggias of the Queen Anne style create an imposing presence out on the treeless Texas prairie. Reminiscent of the set used in the 1950s for the latter-day cowboy movie* Giant, *the Barton House shows the variety of styles included in the American ranch house. It now stands at the Ranching Heritage Center in Lubbock, Texas.*

OPPOSITE: *An architectural plan book provided the design for the Barton House; similar designs might have been found anywhere in the country. The materials, including the mantel's beveled-glass mirror, were ordered back East and came to Texas by train. The parlor and dining room could be separated by sliding doors.*

SUSANNA BIXBY BRYANT RANCH

YORBA LINDA, CALIFORNIA, 1911

This was just the foreman's ranch house; the big house up on the hill was designed for Susanna Bixby Bryant, scion of the southern California ranching dynasty, by architect Wallace Neff along the lines of the King Gillette and Edward Doheny ranches pictured elsewhere in this book.

Yet this simple ranch house is almost a template for many of the first suburban tract ranch houses built forty years later. A simple gabled roof sits over wood board siding; two rock chimneys for the living room and dining room pierce the roof and provide the house's primary source of heat. A porch carved out of one side of the house overlooks the valley. A long, straight corridor extending to the back of the house connects the bedrooms.

In place of Bixby's mansion on the hill, the changing times have covered the newly graded hillside with modern tract houses. Parks, schools, and office parks have replaced the citrus groves of the old Rancho Santa Ana. But squint your eyes and the Craftsman, Adobe, and Victorian-inspired styles of these newcomers become a catalog of American ranch house styles, updated, modernized, and built as if on an assembly line. They are reminders of the appeal that the rural ranch house still holds for the American public. Meanwhile, the old foreman's ranch house, now restored as a museum, sits in their midst.

ABOVE: *Ranch houses were originally lone structures set in isolated sites. But so popular was the image of the ranch that it became the style of choice when the suburbs began to be developed after World War II. Suburban subdivisions were much more densely packed but still allowed residents the opportunity to live on their own small patch of land. Here one can see the contrast of a 1911 ranch house (right) and its descendant, a 1990s suburb. An even larger ranch house, designed for heiress Susanna Bixby Bryant by Wallace Neff, once stood on the upper ridge.*

OPPOSITE: *The pure simplicity of the California ranch house is evident in chimneys made of river stone brought from the nearby stream, Craftsman-style windows, and horizontal board siding.*

ABOVE: *The thick adobe chimney rises above the corrugated tin roof. The materials used in the house are simple, functional, and long-lasting.*

OPPOSITE: *The Navajo rugs once used on the floor have now been moved to the wall, a tribute to their beauty and value. The owner's father purchased them on Arizona's Navajo reservation in the early part of the century. The glass-fronted cabinets hold pots, shards, metates, and other Native American artifacts, many picked up on the ranch itself. Note the red-tinted concrete floors.*

HACIENDA DEL SAN CAYETANO: THE BAILEY RANCH

TUBAC, ARIZONA, 1919

Long before Spanish explorers arrived in the region, a community of some 400 Hohokam Indians lived on the east bank of the Santa Cruz River in present-day Arizona, near what became the Mexican border. Their homes were pit houses, rings dug into the ground and covered by a rough thatch fashioned from willows and cottonwoods growing on the river's banks. The Hohokam lived simply, the men hunting and farming while the women tanned hides and made pots for cooking and storage.

"I'm doing the same thing," says Sarah Bailey, who lives in an authentic ranch house on the same site today. Her father, Weldon Murray Bailey, built the house in 1919 for his own ranching and farming before he married a local schoolteacher, Josephine, and started a family. It sits in a grove of hackberry trees and mesquite. Along with the Hohokam pots and shards that still turn up in the soil after a rain, the mesquite are a reminder of the Indians' successors, the Spanish settlers who once called the site home. Some of the ranch's trees, gnarled with age, date back to their first arrival.

In many ways it is a classic ranch adobe house without the romantic frills. A single gabled roof is still clad in the original corrugated tin. Outdoor living is made easy by the open porch that stretches along the front of the house and by the walled patio at the rear. The thick adobe walls are a practical nod to comfort and climate. A thick buttress supports the adobe chimney. Simple details, native materials. Then as now the house was painted white with dark green trim.

If this is a classic ranch in some ways, it also shows the adaptations and innovations that make the ranch house an ever-changing type. Weldon Bailey remembered his years living in a house in Mobile, Alabama, with French doors overlooking the then crystal-clear bay. Before he married in 1927, he had a vision of a spacious, comfortable house, cool in the summers and warm in the winters, so he lined the porch with eight French doors to let the breeze through. They blend easily with the local adobe.

A lawyer, Weldon had originally come to Tucson early in the century to help resolve a land dispute dating back to Spanish times. The Baca family had been granted a "float," or right to pick a certain number of acres on a large acreage; then squatters moved in, provoking the legal battle. After World War I, Bailey decided to move from Texas to southern Arizona and take up ranching. The land he bought—his holdings eventually grew to 40,000 acres—already had an adobe house as well as a bunkhouse and other out buildings, all dating from before the turn of the century. The bunkhouse still stands.

ABOVE: *Dating from before 1900, the dirt-floored adobe bunkhouse is the oldest structure on the ranch. The tin roof is original.*

OPPOSITE: *The porch served as an outdoor living area for the family. The main parlor is behind the central French doors; there are bedrooms on either end.*

Inside the main house, the lawyer-turned-rancher covered the floors with hand-woven rugs that he had bought while traveling to the Navajo reservation in northern Arizona in 1904. Their deep reds are made from a Pennsylvania dye; even in the exotic West, far from the civilized East, the influence of other parts of the world was felt. The West as an imaginative creation is as much the product of other people and places as of its own indigenous people and materials.

The rugs lay on concrete floors that are themselves a deep, rust-red color. This local color impressed Frank Lloyd Wright so much that he appropriated the color, dubbed Cherokee Red, when he built his house in Scottsdale in 1938. Later he made it a regular part of his home designs. But its roots are in the Arizona ranch house.

Family life took place as much on the front porch as indoors. Here Sarah and her brother, Joseph, played with friends during the day. Here the family gathered after dinner to talk and play games. Here the young folk met and talked to their boyfriends and girlfriends, far enough way from the adults inside for privacy, but near enough for the adults to keep an ear tuned.

The living room anchors the middle of the house. Instead of being part of the wall, the adobe fireplace stands out near the middle of the room, creating a functional space divider between the parlor and the noise and heat of the kitchen. It's a remarkably modern way to organize space.

Flanking either side of the house are large bedrooms. With their ten-foot tongue-and-groove ceilings, they have a luxurious spaciousness that makes them almost contemporary. Windows and French doors on three sides turn each room into an observation deck, with views of mesquite and distant hills in all directions. Stretching out the back of the house in a T are the kitchen and two more bedrooms for the two children. A screen porch, today enclosed with glass, was the only corridor to these rooms. Like the rest of the house, they have doors leading outside and large windows on either side to catch the breeze.

Today the house is no longer intended for an active young family, and the furnishings are simpler. The Navajo rugs are still there, but they have been moved up to the walls as honored decorative pieces. The china cabinets are filled with Hohokam seed, duck, and cooking pots—many found on the ranch—that remind visitors of the vanished residents who lived and worked here for hundreds of years.

OPPOSITE: *French doors bring in sunlight from the walled court. The high ceilings are covered in thin milled strips of wood, a common material in ranches of this era.*

CHAPMAN BARNARD RANCH

PAWHUSKA, OKLAHOMA, 1919

In the movies, a cowboy lives the life of a free-spirited romantic hero, a self-reliant, hardworking, independent loner moving between cantinas, saloons, poker games, and nights under the stars.

At the Chapman Barnard ranch headquarters, built in 1919, the realities of cowboy life are on display. The combination bunkhouse, chow wagon, office, and executive suite is almost Shaker-like in its simplicity. Life here was spare, tough, monastic. Like monks, the cowboys bunked on metal frame cots in small cells and were up before dawn, not especially to pray but to freshen up in the washroom at the end of the arched brick porch before riding the range to their pastures before first light. A pasture could be 10,000 acres in this part of the country—as large as an entire ranch in other states. When the cowboys could get back for lunch, it was served in the common dining room next to the kitchen, where everyone sat at the long refectory table. Only six or eight cowboys worked here most of the year. They made forty dollars a month for their labor, with three days off a year and no benefits. And they had to furnish their own saddles.

ABOVE: *Though built long before the suburban ranch house began to take over the landscape, the Chapman Barnard house has the familiar low lines and sprawling wings that became associated with the later ranch house. Its U-shaped courtyard recalls the basic plan of early Spanish ranchos.*

OPPOSITE: *The stove is new, but the spareness of the clean black-on-white tile floor and counters speaks of the functional nature of this ranch house.*

ABOVE: *The dining hall was the center of cowboy social life. Theirs was a no-frills lifestyle.*

OPPOSITE: *An almost Shaker-like simplicity imbues working ranches like this. This room, originally the ranch office, has concrete floors, a wood-burning fireplace, and the simplest of window frames. The door to the left leads to the two bedrooms used by the owners when they were at the ranch.*

The one-story brick house with two wings was spare and dusty, devoid of frills. Here was the ranch house in its natural habitat, the gently rolling tall-grass prairie of northeast Oklahoma. No shrubs or flowers softened the way it sat on the prairie. Bare light bulbs hung from the center of each room. Gray concrete floors gave way to wood only in the bedrooms used by the bosses, Chapman and Barnard, when they were on site. The house provided only the most meager luxury. Still, in this ground-hugging ranch house, with its porches and simple design, can be seen the low, rambling lines of the suburban ranch house of forty years later.

Oklahoma was still emerging from its isolation as Indian Territory when James Chapman began buying ranch land in 1915. Only thirty miles away, over the Kansas border, ranches settled since the Civil War were smaller. In contrast, the wide-open property of Oklahoma had been saved in trust for a new century and a new era of ranching. By the time Chapman began purchasing land, the auto, steel, and movie industries were consolidating and streamlining. Ranching was heading in the same direction.

Chapman was the ranch's financial deep pockets. Having made a fortune in Oklahoma oil in 1915, he reinvested in ranches. His oil money allowed the ranch to survive the ups and downs of the ranch economy and to expand as good property became available. His brother-in-law, Horace Barnard, managed the ranch, while Chapman lived in Tulsa and only occasionally traveled the long, hard route on rutted roads across the open prairie.

People may only have guessed that James Chapman was one of the wealthiest men west of the Mississippi, but they knew he was shrewd and thrifty. When he arrived at the ranch, he would stay in a simple private room at the end of one wing of the house, sharing the use of a claw-footed bathtub with Barnard. Only the cleaning woman was allowed in the room. When a reunion of cowboys who worked on the ranch was held in the early 1990s, the old ranch hands lined up for their first glimpse of the spartan luxury of the boss's bedroom.

Yet even as ranching turned corporate, there was still room for the romance of the prairie that inspired a thousand cowboy movies. The foreman at the Chapman Barnard until his death in 1952 was Ben Johnson, a man held in awe by all and trusted so thoroughly that he was allowed to be the judge of a race on which he had placed a large bet. This side of the cowboy story was carried on in the movies by Johnson's namesake son, a character actor featured in many westerns.

The Chapman Barnard ranch house has long since ceased to fulfill its original purpose, yet the ranch house still lives as an image. In the same spirit, 38,500 acres of the original ranch are being preserved by the Nature Conservancy, which bought the ranch in 1991. Through science and experiment, the Conservancy is attempting to restore the ecological balance the tall-grass prairie enjoyed before white men arrived. Back then, bison grazed the plains, and Native Americans and lightning set random fires that blazed across the prairie, holding back tree saplings and fertilizing the soil—factors that maintained the diversity and richness of the grassland that once extended through most of the heart of North America. For the last century and a half the great prairie has been pruned back by cities and railroads, farms and ranches, suburbs and freeways.

Today more than 2,000 bison are being reintroduced to the Chapman Barnard ranch. Between the prairie and the ranch house, a fragment of a real ranch lives on.

OPPOSITE: *Owner James Chapman lived in Tulsa, but stayed in this Spartan ranch bedroom when he regularly visited the ranch.*

KIGER RANCH

OSAGE COUNTY, OKLAHOMA, CIRCA 1920

A few miles from the business dynamo of the well-regulated Chapman Barnard Ranch, the Kiger ranch tells another story of cowboy life. It started as a simple shack for a cowboy, probably married. As children arrived, the cowboy added on room after room in a series of gabled additions. This is a family house, located near one of the best water holes in the county, a site enjoyed by generations of the house's occupants during family picnics.

The white board siding—horizontal clapboard here, vertical board and batten there—is set off by the red shingled roof, typical of ranches in this part of the country. But similar to ranches everywhere, it has a porch to lead you outside into the breeze and fresh air.

RIGHT: *A few trees protect the house and the inhabitants of this isolated ranch. The many roof lines represent many additions as the family living here grew.*

OPPOSITE: *Even a larger house would disappear amid the ocean-like swells of the prairie grassland of northeast Oklahoma. The simple gabled design, the roof slightly broken by the porch roof, is the classic ranch house form.*

ROCK CORRAL RANCH

TUMACACORI, ARIZONA, 1926

The Rock Corral Ranch is a ranch out of time. It is still owned and operated by a ranching family that goes back three generations in the region. Unlike the show ranches up on a hilltop, this ranch is tucked down in a small canyon, protected by rock cliffs on three sides. The canyon is a natural corral; Native Americans built their own rock corral on the ranch long before Gene England, a cowboy and pilot from Texas, bought the property in 1931.

Present owner Jean Neubauer's grandfather was another Easterner who found the freedom of the West more to his liking. He migrated to the area after graduating from Harvard in 1902. He built Rancho El Alamo, a castle-like cattle ranch in the Sonoran desert, over the border in Mexico, which lies only fifteen miles away. Though he sent his daughter, Jean's mother, back to Bryn Mawr for school, she returned to Tumacacori and its famous ruined mission, which dates back to 1800. Today Jean continues to run the ranch and the Santa Cruz Chili and Spice Company that her father began as a sideline in 1943.

This is a working ranch, but it has played a role in the film world, too. In 1918 Jean Neubauer's grandmother played a small role in *The Light of Western Stars*, a silent movie starring Winifred Kingston and Dustin Farnum that was filmed in the area. Tom Mix lived nearby, and John Wayne was a guest at the ranch. Visit a few ranches and the line between Hollywood and the Old West soon begins to blur.

The corrals and much of the house are built of river rocks hauled up from the nearby riverbed. In style the ranch house is a throwback to the simple forms of working ranches—direct and purposeful, without the exaggerated stylisms that came to be associated with the cowboy style. But that doesn't mean the house is all work and no play; it has a walled patio where the family puts on a yearly fiesta under the mesquite and eucalyptus trees.

"My ancestors approached life as an adventure," says Jean Neubauer today. As Tucson to the north expands, pressures to change multiply from developers bringing in golf courses and from environmentalists hoping to return the country to nature. Yet she accepts the changes and looks to the future with confidence. "The small family ranch was built on a tradition of hospitality, accommodating a diversity of dreams and purposes. This spirit is very much alive at the Rock Corral Ranch today."

TOP: *The tower room overlooks the walled courtyard— site of many fiestas—and the turquoise tank of an early swimming pool.*

OPPOSITE: *Nestled in a small canyon where the winds blow more gently, the Rock Corral Ranch lives up to its name with a house and nearby corrals made of local stone.*

CROSS BELL RANCH

OSAGE COUNTY, OKLAHOMA, 1926

Not all working ranch houses were austere. E. C. Mullendore and his brother started a family dynasty with the opening of the Cherokee Strip in 1893. The family is heading into the fifth generation, but the ranch house they built in 1926 (old by Oklahoma standards) is a testament to the ever-changing heritage of ranching.

The house was built in the midst of a ranch that spread over more than 100,000 acres. The ranch complex is like a small town. The three-story main house, formal and foursquare, dominates the scene. The main house, the blacksmith shop with its upstairs bunkhouse, the foreman's house, and the smokehouse all are built of the same yellow sandstone quarried on the ranch and common throughout this part of Oklahoma. Nearly 150 horse-drawn wagonloads of rock were needed to build the main house alone.

Finishing off the cluster of active buildings are the stables, barns, corrals, and—an unusual addition to a ranch—a grain elevator. These functional buildings are made of corrugated tin and steel frame, but they blend naturally with the finish and textures of the more formal stone structures.

ABOVE: *Stone for the magnificent three-story house of Oklahoma's Cross Bell Ranch came from the ranch itself. In the initial design, both the first and second stories had open porches; the upper ones were sleeping porches. The ranch's proud brand, displayed throughout the house, appears prominently in the illuminated brand over the front door.*

OPPOSITE: *In an homage to the kind of rustic ornament seen in Buffalo Bill's Pahaska Teepee, the back stairs' balustrades are artfully crafted of natural branches.*

The ranch house began grandly, and it has been expanded over the years, always with careful attention to detail and Western heritage. Originally the house had two front porches; the one upstairs was an open-air sleeping porch. From the start, when this sizable house stood out on the prairie, the family took great care in the architecture. From the piles of cut rocks, the masons selected a number of unusual geologic forms—petrified swirls and pillow-like mounds, shapes molded in the ancient past as mud and sand flowed and were compressed. Today these eye-catching stones pepper the main facade of the house.

Tradition lurks everywhere on the ranch. Ranches like this one must be largely self-sufficient; the ranch blacksmith hammered out the big iron hinges seen throughout the main structures. The cross and bell brand—purchased by the family along with a herd of Mexican cattle over a hundred years ago—appears everywhere. As at some nineteenth-century ranches, the emblem appears right over the front door, translated now into electric lights. Over the living room fireplace (and at the stone-walled horse stables) the stones press outward from the matrix to create the cross and bell. The wallpaper and even the shape of the swimming pool echo the brand.

TOP: *The cross and bell brand appears as a turquoise broach on the mantel's longhorn skull.*

LEFT: *Even the pool takes the shape of the ranch's cross and bell brand.*

OPPOSITE: *The wood-paneled, plank-ceilinged living room is a celebration of the iconic ranch house, from the stone fireplace to the wagon-wheel chandeliers draped in spurs and surmounted by faux-gas lamps. Western-themed paintings and statuary decorate the room.*

The dining room comes closest to a traditional ranch room, with a rock fireplace and hearth at one end and a wood plank ceiling. All four walls are covered with an engaging mural, tooled in linoleum and hand tinted by Craig Sheppard in 1943. The mural depicts a lively panorama of cowboy life against a backdrop of dry mesas and cactus—a scene inspired more by movie westerns than by the grassland of northeastern Oklahoma visible out the front door. Real ranch life and Hollywood ranch life seem to live comfortably side by side.

The living room offers a modernized version of the kind of rustic, hand-hewn lodge room seen at Woolaroc or at Will Rogers' ranch in the 1920s. Here are the wagon-wheel chandeliers, dripping with ornamental spurs, and the rock fireplace. The green, red, and white curtains are a modernized version of colors and patterns from Indian blankets. A coffee table in the shape of the state of Oklahoma, panhandle and all, sits in front of the couch. This is a house well aware of the ranch heritage. It keeps changing, but as it changes it continually updates the Western style.

ABOVE: *Happy roving cowboys, at home on the range, herd the dark clouds out of the sky, keepin' the heavens blue in Craig Sheppard's 1943 tooled linoleum mural that bring the walls of the Cross Bell's dining room to life. The scene of granite spires standing all around amid the sagebrush and the cactus is many miles away from the Oklahoma hills, the land of the great Osage. The mural's prairie sky is wide and high, deep in the heart of Texas or Arizona, where the coyotes wail along the trail and the rabbits rush around the brush. But when the desert sun goes down, this Western image lures us to wander over yonder to see the mountains rise, to ride to the ridge where the west commences, whatever the reality. For when it's twilight and crickets are calling, and coyotes are making a wail, we all want to dream by a smoldering fire along the Navajo Trail. Git along, git hip, little dogies. Yippie ki yo ki yay, yippie ki yo ki yay.*

OPPOSITE: *Once a playroom, now deserted, this room over the ranch's blacksmith shop was originally a bunkhouse.*

DELUXE RANCHOS

THE RICH are different from most of us: they can afford to turn necessities into luxuries. Humble adobes can become mansions, rustic log cabins can become palaces, crudely hand-crafted wood furniture can become a valued aesthetic style filled with romance. Wealthy Westerners transformed the rigors of life on the range into a lavish lifestyle. In the process, the once hardworking ranch turned into a site for relaxation and pleasure. These deluxe ranchos were the predecessors of the populist ranch house of the post–World War II era. Through the magic of gifted architects like Cliff May, the ranch-turned-mansion would become the suburban rancho, everyone's home on the range.

LEFT: *Buffalo Bill, a hero of Phillips, gazes out on a lodge clearly inspired by his own Pahaska Teepee near Yellowstone, built more than twenty years earlier. Phillips' retreat is, however, bigger and more luxurious than Buffalo Bill's.*

ABOVE: *The horn rocker is typical of the self-conscious effort to turn the rustic West into a style.*

OPPOSITE: *The Old West that Phillips toured as a young man is celebrated in the main room of the lodge. It was already disappearing by the time Woolaroc was built, but Phillips wanted to preserve what he remembered of it—though in a highly personalized way.*

WOOLAROC: THE FRANK PHILLIPS RANCH

BARTLESVILLE, OKLAHOMA, 1926
WILLARD DELKS, ARCHITECT

The entry to Woolaroc leads through an idyllic land-scape of fields and trees populated by herds of bison, ostrich, llamas, longhorns, and elk. If Eden had been a ranch, this is what it would have looked like.

Only a man with the wealth of Frank Phillips could afford to build such an idealized ranch. A one-time barber and friend of outlaws, Phillips was the founder of Phillips Petroleum. Like the ranches of other wealthy landowners whose fortunes derived from movies, news-papers, or oil rather than ranching, Woolaroc expresses the trappings and images of the West. Phillips' palatial and rustic ranch is the epitome of this high Western style.

It was Phillips' lover, Sidney Fern Butler, the manager of his New York office, who named the estate Woolaroc (for Woods-Lake-Rocks). The theme of Woolaroc as an idyllic realm is spun out in dozens of details. Through the trees one glimpses teepees made of metal (hide wears out) picturesquely placed on the grounds, which are lighted by concrete lampposts carved to look like saplings. The implied grandeur of the site is set off by an elaborate naturalistic fountain worked into the rock outcroppings that cascade from the lodge down to Lake Clyde. The living rock has been subtly enhanced with steps, waterfalls, and pools of water. Perched above this

TOP: *Frank Phillips.*

LEFT: *Woolaroc Lodge's front door (right) welcomed the rich and famous. Frank Phillips' wealthy East Coast friends had summer homes in Classical and Renaissance styles; Phillips played on the exoticness of the West in creating his personal playground and retreat.*

ABOVE: *The lodge's porch overlooks Lake Clyde. The teepee is one of several Phillips placed for atmosphere around his estate, his personal evocation of the Wild West.*

ABOVE: *Necessity is turned into luxury in this cowboy style. Rough-hewn branches are laboriously crafted into rocking chairs, as if there were no other materials for making furniture in Bartlesville.*

RIGHT: *Frank Phillips housed much of his Western art collection in his home before he decided to found a museum to take care of it on the same site. He opened it to the public long before he died, and it is still a popular destination in Bartlesville. Ever the thoughtful host, Phillips provided fringed and beaded vests like those on the chair so his guests could be properly attired.*

OPPOSITE: *Phillips was not a hunter, but he would occasionally permit a friend to shoot a buffalo on his ranch. Most of the heads displayed in the lodge, however, were part of the exotic collection of animals he imported to Oklahoma. These creatures died natural deaths—if a giraffe could ever be said to have died a natural death in Oklahoma.*

remarkable fountain is the great log lodge, its oversized porch lined with imposing columns twelve feet high. In its way the scene recalls the setting of Italian Renaissance villas. They, too, have their self-consciously rusticated moments.

Woolaroc was Phillips' retreat for friends and business colleagues. He had been a guest at the mansions of the wealthy on the East Coast. He needed a retreat, too, but he molded it in the image of the West. It was not the real West, of course, but the West as he wanted it to be remembered. It was a West that was glorified, romanticized, and turned into a resort, a peaceable kingdom where giraffe could live with buffalo and log cabins could become mansions. No paintings by European masters hung here; instead one sees a portrait of Buffalo Bill. No classical pediments and columns conveyed learning and social status; the lodge's columns are made of logs. At Woolaroc, Phillips and his architect, Willard Delks, who designed Kansas City's innovative Country Club Plaza shopping center, confidently appropriated the image and materials of the West and used them to build a luxurious realm.

The near-magical transformation of the most ordinary and plain artifacts of the West into this Prairie Kingdom can be seen everywhere in the main room of the lodge. It rises more than two stories to heavy log trusses extending across the ceiling. Stone fireplaces stand at each end of the room. Everywhere the eye rests there are reminders of the great outdoors and the mystique of the West as it was being defined in these homes of the rich—in this period still the tastemakers in rustic as well as refined styles.

The space is fairly simple formally, but the natural log walls and the profusion of decoration—animal heads, portraits, Indian blankets, steer horns, handmade rockers, wagon-wheel chandeliers—tell the story. The grand piano is veneered in a thick texture of pine bark. A grandfather clock of thin tree branches stands to one side. Cow-horn chairs rest the body as well as the soul. The whole is an extravaganza of Western materials, artifacts, and styles brought together into a complete vision. From the mighty log trusses to the bronze chandeliers shaped like delicate deer antlers, the room's design is as cohesive as that of any eighteenth-century Robert Adam salon.

In building Woolaroc, Phillips idealized not only the traditional ranch but his own life as well. Born in Nebraska in 1874, Phillips lit out for the territories of Nevada, Colorado, and Utah as a young man. His

roots gave him some right to claim that his house and its museum were "representing the West as I knew it." Returning to Iowa to settle down and marry Jane, a banker's daughter, he found himself in Bartlesville as a banker just as oil was being discovered. Many speculators went broke; Phillips finally hit it rich. He bought ranch land twelve miles from Bartlesville in 1925 and began building the next year with a replica (his mother duly testified) of the log cabin in which he was born. The following year he added an even bigger log cabin.

The Western style at Woolaroc frankly acknowledges its artifice. The porch railings are made of concrete scraped and shaped to the form and texture of branches plucked off a pine tree, much as acanthus leaves and wreaths find their way into marble and wood in Classical ornament. The style was natural for Phillips and other wealthy ranchers; photos of Phillips taken at the ranch

show him wearing a wide-brimmed Stetson, studded chaps, and a holster and bullet belt—along with French cuffs and wire-rim accountant's glasses.

Phillips was not a big-game hunter; the animal heads that crowd the upper reaches of the lodge's main room mostly belonged to animals that lived and died on the ranch itself. Too late for the zebras, Phillips found out that many African species do not take to the Oklahoma climate. The giraffe, on the other hand, fell and broke its neck.

Unlike the Phillipses' Georgian Revival town home in Bartlesville, the master bedrooms here are simple and reflect the Western theme. The rooms connect via a small corridor filled with photos. Frank's room is the smaller; the bed is hand-made of wood imprinted with local brands, including those of the Will Rogers, Phillips, and Cross Bell ranches. McKenney and Hall prints of Indians cover much of the walls, along with portraits of Phillips' mother and father. Next to the easy chair stands an elaborate antler pedestal ashtray decorated with strangely delicate rodent skulls, ungulate teeth, and jawbones.

TOP: *Jane Phillips' bedroom suite was more feminine in decor than Frank's but still featured Indian-pattern rugs and a rustic bedstead.*

LEFT: *Frank Phillips' bedroom was luxuriously spartan. It was a place where a millionaire could enjoy the pleasures of forbearance. The bedstead is burned with the brands of several famous ranches, including the Cross Bell. Prints on the walls include Western themes; the portrait on the right is of his mother.*

OPPOSITE: *Jane Phillips covered her walls with photos of favored male guests to Woolaroc, including Will Rogers, orchestra leader Paul Whiteman, Harry Truman, Rudy Vallee, and a host of business and religious leaders.*

For relaxation in the forest-scented air, French doors lead to a large covered porch that extends the room. Despite the conscious simplicity, the room has a hint of early twentieth-century luxury: the bathroom is fitted with a steam cabinet to help Phillips sweat off the pounds.

Jane's room is even more personalized. Painted in soft blues, the walls are covered with black-and-white photographs of Woolaroc guests—all male—that Jane counted as friends. The images of Will Rogers, Rudy Vallee, Paul Whiteman, and Senator Harry Truman are displayed alongside dozens of businessmen long lost to history. According to curators, the photo gallery was also a rigorous measure of etiquette. Should someone displease Jane, his photo would come off the wall pending appropriate apologies.

Today Woolaroc is open to the public as a museum and nature preserve, as it has been since Phillips himself opened it to the public in 1945, five years before his death. To visit there is to experience the blending of the real and the mythic West. Will Rogers slept here, and Pawnee Bill was a friend who dropped by to stay in one of the nine guest rooms. A portrait of Buffalo Bill hangs on one wall. Woolaroc is one of the ways the image of the Old West—if not the real West itself—lives on.

TOP: *Frank and Jane Phillips and their son John are buried in this mausoleum, which itself grows out of the landscape.*

LEFT: *Phillips saw his executive retreat as an idealized ranch. Buffalo roamed among zebras, ostrich, and llamas.*

OPPOSITE: *Phillips expanded his original retreat with this oversized log cabin, its rustic porch rivaling the grandeur of Mount Vernon. Natural rock outcroppings blend with the landscaped fountains and paving to create a garden that switches easily from artifice to nature and back again.*

Casa Serena: The Bradley Ranch

Colorado Springs, Colorado, 1927
Addison Mizner, architect

Finding a ranch by Addison Mizner in Colorado is a little like finding a cow on a cruise ship: unlikely, but intriguing. The master of Palm Beach magic seems out of place in the foothills of the Rockies.

But one of Mizner's talents was a cinematic ability to conjure up scenes for his clients to live in. In the tropical climate of Florida the scene took the form of high-ceilinged Spanish palaces, usually on the water, or winding *paseos* for strolling shoppers that "recreated" a small Spanish village that never existed. In designing Casa Serena, or the Bradley ranch, for a Florida client with a ranch out west, Mizner explored another Spanish colonial tradition, that of the Southwest. The forms are simpler than in his Florida creations. The U-shaped plan of the rancho provides the basic design; the towers, tiled roofs, chimney caps, and shapely end walls on each wing are composed for maximum effect, like a picture.

ABOVE: *The wrought-iron designs of Mizner's Florida craft shops were adapted to his version of a Western motif. This bell holder features a deer silhouette along with iron work heavily influenced by the Spanish themes of Mizner's Florida architecture.*

OPPOSITE: *Addison Mizner, the master of spaces for society entertaining, created this long formal dining room, though the ceiling is made of rough wood beams to remind visitors that they are in the Wild West.*

ABOVE: *Although Mizner was known for his Spanish-inspired architecture, Casa Serena is more Floridian than Western. It does have the U-shaped courtyard typical of Western ranchos. Casa Serena is Mizner's only work in Colorado.*

RIGHT: *This lamp exhibits the florid hand-crafted detail characteristic of Mizner's designs.*

A two-story porch stands at the head of the courtyard. A low wall and arched wrought-iron gate enclose the far side, creating the feeling of a protected precinct in what was originally a wide-open landscape. Outdoor steps lead up to the tower on one side.

Inside, the slightly overripe Mizner details abound. Ceilings of pecky cypress establish one texture; chandeliers, light sconces, railings—all designed by Mizner—add a sumptuous layer of detail.

Mizner's version of the Southwestern ranch house differs from those of other noted architects. Julia Morgan celebrated the historic form of Mission San Antonio in the Hearst Hacienda. Wallace Neff explored different vernacular traditions, upscaling the form, materials, proportions, ornaments, and spaces as he went along. Mizner, however, is more interested in details, in ceilings and doorways and stairways, with interior effects more than with a strong exterior image.

ABOVE: *The wealthy Doheny family of Los Angeles hired Wallace Neff to build a Spanish rancho on land located between Ojai and Santa Paula. Well acquainted with the style, Neff fitted the house around a courtyard, a plan similar to that of historic Rancho Camulos a few miles away.*

OPPOSITE: *A chapel ends one wing of the house.*

FERNDALE: THE DOHENY RANCH

SANTA PAULA, CALIFORNIA, 1927
WALLACE NEFF, ARCHITECT

In 1929 Wallace Neff would create a full-blown Hollywood extravaganza at the King Gillette Ranch. He pursued a different direction when he designed this earlier ranch house for the oil-rich Doheny family of Los Angeles along the winding road to Ojai. Like many of the wealthy, the Dohenys had a cattle ranch as part of their portfolio, though the startling beauty of the site and of the house in its glen suggest it was as much a retreat as a working ranch.

Here Neff moved toward the simplicity of the original haciendas of California while showing how that chaste vernacular style could be adapted to create an appropriate home for a wealthy family. The ranch house sits on the floor of a landscaped forest glade, next to a stream. Oaks, redwoods, maples, and palms create an almost complete canopy over the house, though the backdrop of majestic mountains can still be glimpsed.

Like the original haciendas, this house is as much a collection of several small buildings as a single big building. The room wings, the chapel, the living room,

and the study all are self-contained and connected only by the broad tile roof and the outdoor *corredors* and breezeways. In a ranch house, the out-of-doors is never more than a few steps away.

The house wraps around three sides of a rectangular courtyard, as did Rancho Los Cerritos (pictured later in this chapter). Beneath a covered colonnade the rooms open directly onto the court. Instead of adobe, the walls are made of whitewashed brick. The brick's rough texture adds to the feeling of a house built simply and crudely, like the authentic ranchos. Neff adds touches, however, that the original haciendas could rarely afford, and rarely needed. Wrought-iron box grilles cover each window along the bedroom wing, allowing the sash to open out. A picturesque iron gate and gate house sit by the main road.

This is, no question, a high-style version of the ranch house. But in its courtyard, in its long bedroom wings, and in the low line of the tiled roof can be seen the outline of the suburban ranch house that Cliff May would create from the same original sources in a few years.

ABOVE: *The chapel's apse provides an opportunity for a semicircular trellis.*

OPPOSITE: *Wrought-iron grates over the windows—set out from the wall of the house to allow windows to be left open at night—are a feature more of Spanish architecture than of the simpler California ranchos. The rancho sits in a fern dale at the foot of rugged mountains.*

ABOVE: *Architect John Byers was an expert in adobe construction and built several houses in the material. Authenticity of both method and effect was critical to him; unlike the designers of the refined stylings of the Hearst, Doheny, and Gillette ranches, Byers kept his design authentically simple.*

OPPOSITE: *Looking almost like a movie set, the Kemper Campbell ranch has been weathered to perfection. It sits in the high desert above Los Angeles. The living room is the two-story block. During the Depression, the working ranch became a dude ranch and was popular with many Hollywood celebrities.*

KEMPER CAMPBELL RANCH

VICTORVILLE, CALIFORNIA, 1929
JOHN W. BYERS, ARCHITECT

Credit architect John Byers' eye for the difficulty you'll have telling whether this is an authentic nineteenth-century adobe or a twentieth-century replica. You won't be the first to be puzzled. Jean Campbell DeBlasis, daughter of Kemper and Litta Belle Campbell, says that people had the same reaction when the house was brand-new in 1929.

Unlike Wallace Neff and Julia Morgan, and their romantic fantasias based on the ranch house, Byers studied traditional adobe construction techniques and used them in a series of houses in Santa Monica and Palm Springs (though not in the 1936 medieval-style home he designed for Shirley Temple's parents in Beverly Hills). Here, the straight-line plan of the house and the exposed adobe walls have the simplicity of a prospector's desert shack, while the high walls recall the plain proportions of the Camulos adobe.

The adobe walls have always been exposed, without the layer of whitewashed mud plaster that is often applied. Strands of the straw used to bind the adobe mud can be seen embedded in the brown matrix of the walls' weathered surface. The wooden board-and-batten walls and heavy timber porch columns and beams have been dried and conditioned by the high desert climate. Even today the Campbell family must take care to keep

water away from the walls by making sure that the wide eaves stay in good condition and that the drainage ditches work ("Grab your shovels," Kemper Campbell would call when cloudbursts threatened).

The Campbells were not wealthy like Hearst, Gillette, or Doheny, but they still wanted a ranch retreat for escape from their Los Angeles home and their jobs as lawyers. They found an old ranch in Victorville, in the high Mojave desert several hours' drive up the Cajon Pass. There they raised cattle and milk cows, and grew alfalfa and other crops. When the Depression reduced disposable income, many friends in Los Angeles asked if they could come to the ranch for a reasonably priced vacation. On the working ranch, a dude ranch was born: five dollars a day or twenty-five dollars a week, meals included.

Not only attorney and judicial friends came. Will Rogers slept here. A friend of the Campbells, he quartered some of his polo ponies on the ranch and gave them to the Campbell kids when he retired them. Family tradition recalls that Rogers liked the two-story living room so well that he literally raised the roof at his house, adding a balcony and guest rooms upstairs.

ABOVE: *A balcony overlooks the main living room, a gathering place for family and dude ranch guests.*

OPPOSITE: *The bedrooms of the main house overlook the two-story living room. The corner beehive fireplace is typical of adobe houses, although the craftsmanship of this one is especially extraordinary.*

Other Hollywood celebrities visited also, including George Burns and Gracie Allen, Louis Calhern, and Clark Gable. Producers once sent Herman Mankiewicz to the Campbell spread to finish the script for *Citizen Kane* because they knew that liquor was banned from the ranch. Another literary light who visited here was British author J. B. Priestley. After spending a vacation at the ranch, Priestley returned to England to write *Midnight on the Desert*.

The house that welcomed these illustrious guests was truer than most deluxe ranchos to the architecture of authentic ranches. Byers created a warm, sturdy home for the desert, but he made little effort to romanticize the house. A tall brick fireplace stands in a living room notable for its simplicity and severity. Overlooking the room is a wood plank balcony. The wood stairs on one side originally had no railing, a suggestion of the austere life of real ranches.

Off the living room is a dining room with a low plank ceiling from which oil lanterns are suspended. There are touches of luxury here, but they are those that might be found in the ranch home of a well-educated cattleman. (In fact, one of the Campbells' sons attended St. Johns College, Oxford, and their daughter attended the Sorbonne.) A china cabinet features doors fashioned from a Chinese screen painted on wood. A four-inch ledge circling the room atop the wainscoting is inlaid with hand-painted tiles. The tiles are a mark of the way Byers attended to detail while staying well within the vocabulary of the ranch house style.

ABOVE: *A sombrero hangs over the fireplace.*

OPPOSITE: *Once an open porch with an outdoor barbecue, this room was enclosed when the ranch became a dude ranch in the 1930s.*

KING GILLETTE RANCH

CALABASAS, CALIFORNIA, 1929
WALLACE NEFF, ARCHITECT

It's amazing what selling enough razor blades can buy.

Drive far enough along Mulholland Highway out of Calabasas and around the curve of a hill, and a small valley opens up beneath you. On a rise in the center of the valley stands a rambling hacienda of white stucco. Stately towers rise, wings sprawl over the landscape, bungalows and a stable with a circular tower appear amid the oak trees on the valley floor.

Built for King Camp Gillette, inventor of the safety razor, this rancho deluxe is an ideal vision of a Spanish grandee's estate. It is as carefully plotted as a tracking shot in the hands of a Hollywood master. Your windshield acts as a film camera's viewfinder as you drive down the tree-lined road past the stables, over a white stuccoed bridge, through the manicured lawn, and under a giant archway in one wing before swinging around to the car court and the front entry of the main house.

The approach lets you see the ranch from every angle—and to be mightily impressed. Stand back for a long shot and you see it against the rugged Santa Monica Mountains rising in the distance. Stand close and you see the imported tile work that tells its own story.

This is the sort of rancho depicted in the romance movies. It has the picturesque lushness of the home Hollywood imagined for *Ramona* in the 1936 film version of Helen Hunt Jackson's classic novel of old California—a far cry from the simpler Rancho Camulos that was Jackson's actual inspiration. Here, fountains drip water into tiled pools. Outdoor stairs lead up to wooden balconies. Richly wrought iron grilles cast delicate shadows in the moonlight on the gleaming white walls and protect boudoir windows open to the night air. There is hardly a trace of rusticity in Neff's version of ranch life other than the casual way the building's wings sprawl over the hill. This is a home for the landed gentry.

Gillette did not enjoy his Hollywood-perfect estate for long. His fortune was wiped out in the stock market crash of 1929; he died three years later. The house was sold, fittingly, to a Hollywood producer, who allowed Gillette's wife to live on in one of the estate's bungalows.

TOP: *Architect Neff lavished attention on the ranch's stables, which continued the idyllic Spanish scene with a massive tower complete with picturesque dove cotes.*

OPPOSITE: *For a millionaire like King Gillette, a ranch was one of many homes and more of a showplace than a place of work. By the 1920s ranches had become a status symbol, and Wallace Neff's design turns the country ranch into a sybaritic paradise fit for a movie set.*

TOP: *After its 1930 remodeling, Rancho Los Cerritos became a mansion for a Bixby family scion. The portico was glassed in as a sun room. The roof, which originally was flat and later was shingled, was tiled in picturesque Spanish tiles, a conceit influenced more by Hollywood than by history. The courtyard, typical of early California ranchos and once the work yard of the house, became a landscaped garden.*

OPPOSITE: *Today a gate encloses the courtyard.*

RANCHO LOS CERRITOS

LONG BEACH, CALIFORNIA, 1844
(REMODELED, 1930)

Some historic ranches are in ruins; it takes a skillful imagination to rebuild the walls and replace the roof in the mind's eye in order to see what the ranch looked like in its heyday. Rancho Los Cerritos requires the opposite skill: to strip away some of the well-meaning additions from the 1930s to see what it was like in 1844, when it served as headquarters for a 27,000-acre cattle ranch.

Imagine a flat roof on the adobe walls. Instead of the peaceful courtyard garden of flowers and fountains, imagine a dirt area where workers unload sacks of grain from wagons, horses are brought in for reshoeing by the blacksmith, and the smells of cooking waft from the kitchen. On a self-sufficient rancho, courtyards were functional work spaces rather than restful gardens.

Photos from the early twentieth century show the ranch in decay. Pigs roam through the ramshackle courtyard; an abandoned car lies on its side. The rancho owes its revival in 1930 to Llewellyn Bixby, and architect Kenneth Wing. Bixby's father, Lewellyn, and his cousins Thomas and Benjamin Flint bought the rancho from original owner, John Temple, in 1866, but the family abandoned their one-time headquarters and homestead for plusher neighborhoods in the 1880s. A half-century later, the younger Llewellyn decided to move back in. But he did not choose to restore the ranch to its 1844 condition, nor to its condition in 1872, when the family added a steep shingled gable atop the flat roof. Instead he remodeled it in the style of the fashionable Spanish

Colonial revival of the 1920s. He took history and edited it, much like a movie, and turned the family homestead into a romantic and extremely attractive vision of life in old California.

Today a glimpse of the early life of the rancho is possible indoors, where several rooms have been restored as a museum. The doors are low and tilting; the rooms are small and the walls thick. The wide two-story porch extending the length of the garden side still provides welcome relief in the hot days of summer.

In other ways the restoration tells a story, not of a real past, but of a time that has been fictionalized and romanticized. Over the bones of the old rancho, a rancho deluxe has been created. The gently sloping roof features tiles laid in heavy, wavy rows as a mark of the tile-layer's hand, emphasizing a love for the irregularities of hand crafting. The workaday courtyard of the 1840s has become a pleasant garden with a glass sun porch along one side. The common style of the nineteenth century has been adorned; its common spaces have been glorified. Pieces of the rancho past fit into the new story and are kept; other pieces are edited out. This is one way the rancho lives on long after its original use has vanished.

ABOVE: *Built by Anglos but rooted firmly in the Hispanic style of California's Mexican culture, Rancho Los Cerritos shows the genteel grace of a prosperous landowning family. Ornate Victorian chairs and a delicate print wallpaper mark this as a special room for social occasions. Thick walls meant small windows; the porch beyond cut the sunlight and heat even more.*

RIGHT: *The blacksmith shop was one of the utilitarian facilities incorporated in the courtyard wings of the rancho.*

OPPOSITE: *Today restored as a museum, this room gives a better idea of the original appearance of a room at Rancho Los Cerritos. Hard-backed chairs and chamber pots were among the few conveniences.*

The Hearst Hacienda

JOLON, CALIFORNIA, 1930
JULIA MORGAN, ARCHITECT

In the midst of building La Casa Encantada, his hilltop home at San Simeon, William Randolph Hearst decided he needed a headquarters nearer to the center of his cattle ranch. The huge ranch he inherited from his father and mother stretched along much of central California's coast and inland valleys. The ranch headquarters were to include a foreman's home, bunkhouse, and stables as well as accommodations for Hearst and his guests when they rode over from San Simeon, about 25 miles away as the crow flies. He asked his hardworking architect, Julia Morgan, to design it. By any normal standards the hacienda would qualify as a mansion; by Hearst standards it was modest. Morgan quietly added it to the demands of building one of the most complex and technically challenging construction projects of the 1920s.

For the design of the house, client and architect chose to copy the 1771 Mission San Antonio de Padua in Jolon. It was appropriate enough for a mission to serve as a model for a ranch; though missions were churches, they were also headquarters for farming and herding operations. Built on a hilltop overlooking Mission San Antonio, today the hacienda is often mistaken for the mission.

Although the hacienda reflected the mission's square courtyards and arcaded porches, Morgan turned the design into a more modern, more complex Beaux Arts plan. An open-air arcade is the spine and main path from the residences on one side to the dining room, kitchen, and lounge on the other. In the tradition of adobes like Rancho Camulos, the kitchen is separated from the rest of the building. Wings stretch out along this spine, and the courts created between them each have an individual character. For the face of each wing Morgan borrowed Mission San Antonio's unique detached facade— a delicate piece of brickwork showing off a Baroque silhouette against the plain wall and wood gable roof of the sanctuary. The hacienda is topped by a dome on one end and a balancing square tower on the other.

Hearst called his opulent San Simeon castle "the ranch." That famous structure has long overshadowed the more modest Jolon ranch house, tucked away in a valley on what is now Fort Hunter-Liggett, where the tawny hills and gnarled oaks have changed little since the days of the ranchos.

ABOVE: *Morgan's design at San Simeon gave the main house the appearance of a Spanish cathedral; here she took elements from the humbler mission of San Antonio de Padua nearby. The dining room wing with the square tower is on the right.*

OPPOSITE: *Willliam Randolph Hearst's family fortune was based on mining, but he translated it into a true twentieth-century wealth of newspapers and information. His "other" ranch, inland from San Simeon, translated the simple ranch house into a glorification of the Spanish mission style.*

ABOVE: *The one-story wing on the left is the living room; the two-story wing includes a kitchen on the first floor and bedrooms above.*

OPPOSITE: *A 1930s vision of a ranch has been reinterpreted in the living room by the present owners. They restored brick walls and wood ceilings and redecorated to highlight the rancho design themes.*

RANCHO DIABLO

LAFAYETTE, CALIFORNIA, 1930
LILLIAN BRIDGMAN, ARCHITECT

The character of a building often resides in its ornament. Rancho Diablo's iron door latches, built-in hutches, festive bathroom tiling, and ceramic medallions possess the spirit of delight and celebration of a faraway hacienda in long-ago California.

But Rancho Diablo is no nineteenth-century hacienda. It is a second-generation rancho, one of the manifestations of California's rediscovery of its Hispanic past in the first half of the twentieth century, just as the Craftsman style was opening the eyes of many architects to the joys of handcrafting and rustic finishes.

The house was built in 1930 by the father of tennis star Helen Wills. She inherited it and later willed it to a university, but the house was decrepit when Ace Architects took on the task of breathing life back into Berkeley architect Lillian Bridgman's design.

The restored house has been revitalized as a suburban residence. The front facade is a mix of two-story hacienda (brick below, wood above) with a one-story wing balanced by a tall chimney. The facade evokes memories of the fortress-like security found in some haciendas; walk through the heavy wood doors and you are in a sheltered passageway. Secondary doors lead from here to the fireplace room to the left, and to the kitchen and the steps upstairs to the right. Walk straight ahead and you find yourself in the garden, looking out at the view of distant Mt. Diablo.

ABOVE: *A dining-room sideboard designed by the architect, Lillian Bridgman.*

RIGHT: *Victorian furniture and Indian rugs typical of early ranches mingle with paintings of Western themes from a later period when ranchers became more self-conscious about being in a place that could be stylized as Western.*

OPPOSITE: *A built-in cabinet with Mexican Day of the Dead artifacts provides the backdrop for cowskin lounge chairs selected by the owners.*

In their renovations, Ace made the breezeway more comfortable by enclosing it with glass doors. But from there they embellished, rejuvenated, and intensified the original spirit of the place. Typical of their efforts is the garden, which became a showcase of cactus enchantments, an arboretum of different species and multicolored blossoms, a symbolic re-creation of the archetypal Western landscape.

In the fireplace room the furnishings and ornament take the house's original homage to the old hacienda in new directions. Specially selected cowhides cover the lounge chairs. Side pieces by Wyoming furniture designer Thomas Molesworth—half cowboy, half Deco—stand against the walls. Over the fireplace a ceramic mosaic shows a sombreroed guitar player romancing a Spanish dancer, a motif common to both tourist trinkets and songs in the Southwest. The music, the balmy air, and the gracefully ruined adobe walls of Old Spain come to life in that tile picture and in the ranch house itself.

ABOVE: *The central breezeway, enclosed by the owners with folding glass doors on the left, has entries to the kitchen (shown), the living room, and the stairs to the bedrooms.*

RIGHT: *The expansive second-story Monterey Colonial balcony (through door to left) running the length of the house is only a few steps from the bedrooms.*

OPPOSITE: *The built-in cabinets are original to the dining room-kitchen area.*

ABOVE: *Board-and-batten redwood paneling, typical
of both early ranches and Bay Area Craftsman architecture,
covers the walls of this upstairs bedroom.*

OPPOSITE: *A bedroom fireplace.*

RIGHT: *Rancho Diablo enjoys a view of distant Mount Diablo.*

BELOW: *The two-story Monterey Colonial-style porch looks out on the cactus garden, a favorite lounging spot for Trigger. The horseshoe tables and chairs are designed by the owners.*

OPPOSITE: *The Monterey Colonial balcony provides the backdrop to the backyard cactus garden planted by the current owners.*

KENYON RANCH

TUBAC, ARIZONA, 1935

Even movie stars who didn't appear in westerns—not to mention ordinary folk—could play cowboy during vacations at dude ranches like the Kenyon Ranch south of Tucson. The horses were real, but so was the maid service.

Fred and Sis Allen opened the Kenyon in 1935. The house is low and unimposing, seemingly sinking into the earth as the chaparral grows higher to hide it. The main entry is through a windowless stone wall. Except for the small bell tower rising over the wood door, it looks like the entrance to an old fort. But step through the plank door and you realize you are no longer in the harsh and dangerous West. You are in a garden. A shady L-shaped porch frames two sides of a lawn and embraces a spectacular view of the dry valley and craggy Santa Rita mountains. In the mid twentieth century, people had the time and money to enjoy views like this. The view becomes part of the architecture. We've exited the West of the hardscrabble struggle for survival and entered the West of relaxation and rejuvenation amid awesome scenery in the clear desert air.

Inside, the rooms step up here, down there, following the undulations of the ground. The ranch is filled with self-conscious Western stylisms, like the piping and embroidered broncos on Gene Autry's shirts. Tin cutouts of broncos and saguaros ornament the knotty-pine wet bar at the pool house. A line of cowboy boots in all sizes hangs from the beams of the tack room.

ABOVE: *Reminiscent in part of a mission and in part of a fort, the stone wall of the ranch separated the gravel forecourt from a shady and delightful patio just inside.*

OPPOSITE: *Graveled courtyards are scattered among the casitas, the guest rooms for this dude ranch.*

TOP: *The small casitas, or guest bungalows, each had their own porch and fireplace. City dudes came to this ranch for relaxation—exactly the opposite of the experience of cowboys on working ranches.*

OPPOSITE: *This kitchen served up to forty guests a day for breakfast, lunch, and dinner.*

Half motel, half ranch, the Kenyon ranch clustered a dozen casitas, or guest bungalows, around an intimate courtyard. Meals were served in the large dining room flanked by two fireplaces. A big kitchen handled the restaurant duties, but also was as charming as the cozy parlors and sun porch where guests played card games. The dude ranch is a series of delightful spaces for a floating cocktail party.

The casitas are furnished sparely, but they have fireplaces to warm the soul. Before spas and fat farms, tourists still expected a bit of rustic rigor in their ranch vacation. That would change later in the century, when luxury would reign.

The Kenyon is far from a traditional Western homestead, but it is a compelling twentieth-century ranch. Here ranch architecture and the ranch experience have been refined, edited, and repackaged. The wooden horse trough of tradition has transmuted into a turquoise swimming pool. The landscape is the same as the Old West's, but it is reconceived as an attraction, not an obstacle. The hard business of ranching has given way to the modern industries of tourism and entertainment that use the old landscapes and motifs to attract urban dwellers in search of new places and new experiences.

ABOVE: *Now part of a private residence, the Kenyon Ranch dining room was once filled with dining tables.*

LEFT: *Though not as Spartan as an actual bunkhouse, dude ranch guest rooms offered guests the spirit of clean, simple living with varnished wood furnishings, plank ceilings, and stone fireplaces.*

OPPOSITE: *One of the sitting rooms where guests played cards or chatted now includes matched Gothic-style cabinets flanking the doorway.*

CHAPTER 3
MEDIA COWBOYS

FROM BUFFALO BILL'S Wild West Show to Owen Wister's novel *The Virginian* to William S. Hart's and John Wayne's celluloid cowboys, twentieth-century America redefined the West—and itself—in the mass media. The mass media in turn shaped America by reflecting the way the country liked to see itself: rugged, plain, independent, free. Nowhere was that interplay of image and reality more apparent than in the homes of cowboy movie stars. There the true West was edited and concentrated into the idealized homestead of the self-made man. It was an exceedingly attractive image, but it was also very far from the real ranches of the prairies.

LEFT: *This cowboy-style extravaganza by one of America's best-known cowboys mixes cleverly designed rustic charm with an almost museum-like care for artifacts. In contrast to the formal mansions of the wealthy and famous back East—or in nearby Beverly Hills—Will Rogers made a virtue of simplicity: comfortable chairs, Indian blankets used as throw covers or to add color to a banister. Practical equipment like spurs, riding tack, and powder horns are used ornamentally. It all looks casual and yet it is knowingly and thoroughly combined to create a complete style.*

ABOVE: *Friends of Lummis, including Native Americans from New Mexico pueblos, raised the stone and concrete walls of El Alisal. Like Julia Morgan thirty years later at the Hearst ranch at Jolon, Lummis used California missions as inspiration for the style of his arroyo house.*

OPPOSITE: *Searching for a new way to design a Western home when Victorian was the popular style, Lummis combined both new and old elements. The thick concrete walls echoed the adobe walls of the early ranchos. Hand-made doors—with inventive, protomodern geometric glass frames—imitated the do-it-yourself necessities of homes on the range. The flickering candlelight from niches on the wall (left) created a chapel-like intimacy for lively dinner parties with artists, authors, and the famous.*

EL ALISAL: THE CHARLES FLETCHER LUMMIS RANCH

LOS ANGELES, CALIFORNIA, 1898–1912

If the West was in part invented by the East, Charles Fletcher Lummis was one of the first Easterners to give it a try.

The impulse to throw off the formalities of life in the East has always been part of the appeal of ranches. Kick back, keep things simple, track dirt inside. Live among noble natives and amidst surroundings conducive to the quiet, devotional life of the mission friars.

Although it was not a working ranch, El Alisal began the canonization of natural materials and simple qualities that were this Harvard graduate's vision of Western life. He built the house with his own hands, helped by the hands and strong backs of Anglo and Native American friends, between 1898 and 1912.

El Alisal's design was a mixture of mission, Crafts-man style, adobe, and fort. Above all the house was a place for social life. One-time librarian for the city of Los Angeles, founder of groups to preserve both Native American culture and historic buildings (then slightly less historic than they are now), Lummis loved to enter-tain. The dining room is a convivial dining hall from a monastery with concrete walls as smooth and shapely as walls made of adobe. Niches hold candles to create

ABOVE: *Every log for the ceiling was placed by hand; every cabinet, door, and window frame was designed, made, and set by hand. Lummis was a romantic fighting against the many changes overwhelming the old way of rancho life.*

LEFT: *Part of Lummis' collection of Pueblo Indian pottery was displayed on the mantel shelves above the fireplace. Consciously crude and handmade, the unfinished logs and hand-hammered copper (protecting the logs from fire) showed the way to a new aesthetic for the West.*

OPPOSITE: *Lummis admired the outdoor life of the early ranchos and recreated it in the shaded veranda on the edge of the courtyard. The height of the low walls is perfect for seating.*

an atmosphere of far away and long ago. On the warm afternoons and balmy evenings along the Pasadena Arroyo, Lummis' friends could gather in the outdoor patio. A porch supported by peeled log posts shelters one side; a low bench invites guests to sit and chat. A large willow overhangs the space, bordered by a guest house (where Lummis invited his previously unsuspected illegitimate daughter to live when she showed up as an adult). The tower held Lummis' private quarters, which were accessible by way of a ladder that had to be lowered from above.

Lummis was never a cowboy, but he came by his knowledge of the West honestly. In 1885 he walked from Chillicothe, Ohio, where he ran a newspaper, to Los Angeles, where he accepted a job with the *Los Angeles Times*. On the way he stopped off in New Mexico, where he made friends; he returned there many times in his life. Once out west, he devoted the same effort to learning the Tiwa language as he had to learning Latin and Greek at Harvard.

El Alisal is Lummis' reinterpretation of the old adobe ranchos and missions he visited and admired. But it is also stamped with his bias, his romantic vision. As a historian he did his best to create a convincing story to explain and give purpose to life in the West; as the architect of his own home, he sought to give that story form. The Western myth would eventually stray far from Lummis' educated and passionate ideal. By 1898, the Wild West shows were already creating an invincible myth that would be further developed by Hollywood. But Lummis can take credit for beginning the transformation of the Western hacienda into an architectural icon.

ABOVE: *W. F. Cody, known as "Buffalo Bill."*

OPPOSITE: *The lodge's bar room flanks the two-story main room. Even in this self-consciously rustic, crudely handmade construction, the placement of random-sized logs adds a rugged rhythm to the style.*

PAHASKA TEEPEE: THE BUFFALO BILL LODGE

EAST ENTRANCE OF YELLOWSTONE PARK, WYOMING, 1904

When Colonel William F. Cody, called Buffalo Bill, and his fellow investors began to move into Wyoming's Bighorn Basin in 1895, it was one of the last large uninhabited areas in the West. Bill had already turned the rugged life of the West into a national myth and a national entertainment. He then helped to make it the basis of the new industry of tourism.

"Buffalo Bill's Hotels in the Rockies" were advertised nationwide. In 1902 Bill opened the Irma Hotel, named for his daughter, in Cody, the new town named for himself. Two years later he built his own hunting lodge between Cody and Yellowstone Park. Traveling as much as he did with his show and for other purposes, he probably used the lodge a half dozen times at most; the rest of the time it was used as an inn. Just before he died in 1917, he was considering turning the working ranch he had bought in the Bighorn Basin south of Cody in 1895, the TE, into a dude ranch. The new wealth of the West lay in tourism as much as in cattle and minerals.

These operations were part of Cody's business empire, which was funded by the profits from his Wild West shows of the 1890s. He never quite stabilized his fortune, though. In 1909 he merged his show with Pawnee Bill's Wild West show, but by 1913 the combined operation went bankrupt and closed.

Cody still managed to entertain everyone from Theodore Roosevelt to Frederic Remington to Prince Albert I of Monaco in style at his hunting lodge, which was designed by his friend Archibald Anderson. Named Pahaska Teepee ("Long Hair's Lodge") by a Native American friend, the rustic base camp was built around a free-standing chimney made of river stone. The rest of the structure was constructed from unpeeled lodgepole pine logs stacked together in a deliciously crude manner. Unlike the straight and true logs of the earlier OW Ranch in Montana, less than two hundred miles east, the Pahaska Teepee's logs are rough and irregular, purposely emphasizing the appearance of primitive construction. This was the home of a mountain man, a man who has had the polish of civilization rubbed away. But it was considerably more than a simple rancher's homestead: thirteen small bedrooms are tucked under the second-story eaves.

The lodge's main room also reflected Cody's unique mixture of the authentic and mythic. Skins decorated the wall; the sightless eyes of elk heads peered down from the gloom of the two-story space. But so did posters and advertisements for Buffalo Bill himself. The lodge was a stage set, a way to both retain and enhance some of the character of the original wilderness experience that was fast giving way to tourism and the managed wildness of national parks like Yellowstone.

TOP: *Built on the road to the east entrance to the new tourist attraction of Yellowstone Park, Pahaska Teepee sits under towering cliffs.*

LEFT: *Buffalo Bill embarked on hunting parties from this lodge with friends like Theodore Roosevelt and Prince Albert of Monaco. Famous or not, guests stayed in one of the thirteen small rooms on the second floor.*

ABOVE: *Buffalo Bill's Wild West shows helped create and spread the aura of glamor, excitement, and romance we associate with the West. At his hunting lodge near his Wyoming ranch, he helped create a romantic image of the rustic Western home. The log cabin of peeled logs, ornamented with animal heads and skins, had the bravura of a rugged frontier life but was far from the sedate Victorian furnishings preferred by most actual ranchers.*

ABOVE: *Portraits of Native American friends of Buffalo Bill, some of whom toured with his Wild West Show, line the dining room walls.*

OPPOSITE: *Buffalo Bill was one of the first of the media figures who adopted this rustic style out of choice rather than necessity.*

BLUE HAWK PEAK: THE PAWNEE BILL RANCH

PAWNEE, OKLAHOMA, 1910

By 1908 Mae Lillie had had enough of touring with the Wild West show run by her husband, Gordon William Lillie, better known as Pawnee Bill. She especially didn't want to tour with Bill's new partner, the unreliable William F. Cody. So this one-time Philadelphia Quaker, Smith College graduate, and erstwhile horseback sharp-shooter (some say she was better than Annie Oakley) decided to retire from show business and build a proper home for an Eastern woman in the heart of Oklahoma.

Pawnee Bill went back on the road, joining his show with Buffalo Bill's fiscally precarious Wild West Show. Ringling Brothers would do the same with Barnum and Bailey. Metro, Goldwyn and Mayer would combine as MGM. Chevrolet, Buick, Cadillac, Pontiac, and Oldsmobile would join forces as General Motors. It was a time of mergers, and the myth and entertainment industry was no exception. Meanwhile, Mae went to work on her new residence on the prairie.

TOP: *Gordon Lillie, called Pawnee Bill.*

LEFT: *The stylized ornament at the peak of the roof and the natural stone arcade reflect the Craftsman style that was then fashionable. Buffalo used to wander up to this porch.*

OPPOSITE: *Coffered wood ceilings, inlaid wood floors, a grand piano, and a silver martini mixer were some of the sophisticated accoutrements of the Blue Hawk Peak Ranch. The ceramic mosaic over the fireplace depicts a buffalo herd.*

Mae built her mansion on a treeless hilltop near the Pawnee reservation where her husband had moved in 1875 at the age of fifteen. (He had been a teacher and interpreter on the reservation, and it was there that he acquired the name Pawnee Bill.) The Lillies had bought the 5,000-acre ranch a few years earlier from a Pawnee friend, a medicine man named Blue Hawk, and they named the ranch Blue Hawk Peak. Nearby stood a mud lodge, the traditional residence and meeting place for the Pawnee. Covered with a thick layer of dirt over a wood frame, it was some seven feet high. Bill and Mae themselves lived in a log cabin with a dirt floor until they moved into the new house. Next to these humble homes, the two-story ranch house, built of wood and covered in heavily textured stucco dashed with rocks, was an otherwordly sight on the then treeless prairie.

Since then trees have grown as the local ecology changed. Today the Craftsman-style house, with its wide eaves and diagonal air vents at the peaks of the roofs—a design perhaps borrowed from a woven Indian rug, as were the inlaid wood patterns trimming the living room floor—seems quaint and comfortable on the edge of the small town of Pawnee. But in 1910 this $100,000 home was about as incongruous as the palace of Versailles would be in the Sahara Desert. With no fences to stop them, the ranch's bison ambled up to the front porch, where the Nouvea-uinfluenced ceramic tile trim depicted—what else?—bison on the plains. Only the fine mahogany doors kept the animals from wandering inside.

ABOVE: *Mae and Gordon Lillie lived in this log cabin on Blue Hawk Ranch while they awaited the completion of the ranch house.*

OPPOSITE: *With dirt floors, log walls, and chamber pots, the log cabin was a far cry from the wood-paneled luxury of the Lillies' future home—but closer to the reality of many pioneers' ranches.*

Mae's taste is evident inside in the dark wood paneling and in the Doric columns flanking the formal living room. Sumptuous embossed wallpaper covered the walls above the wood wainscot; glass bookcases in the living room held the complete works of Carlyle, Hugo, and Goethe. Fine china and stained glass ornamented the dining room, whose walls were hung with tapestries. The soft blue-green master bedroom on the ground floor had a delicate stenciling around the cornice line. An indoor water closet and a separate china wash basin with running water were great luxuries here.

In 1916 the Lillies adopted a son; in another overlap with the Old West, he had traveled on an orphan train from Chicago to Oklahoma, where abandoned children were shipped out to open country to start new lives. In 1925 he died in a play accident at their home; his train set, clip-on roller skates, and Tinker Toys can still be seen in his playroom under the upstairs eaves.

TOP: *The public rooms on the main floor contrasted polished paneling and carved ornament that could be found in most fine Eastern homes with paintings and inlaid mosaics depicting Western themes. The view is from the living room through the entry hall to the study.*

LEFT: *Luxurious wallpaper imitates hand-tooled leather.*

OPPOSITE: *In his study Pawnee Bill surrounded himself with mementos of his friends and career. The stuffed alligator standing by the fireplace had been part of his show; it lived in a pond outside the back door. Although the room's style is the height of Eastern taste in its dark wood and crown moldings, the mosaic in the mantel shows a distinctly Western scene of Native Americans. The chairs are influenced by the Arts and Crafts style.*

ABOVE: *Pawnee Bill's ranch was astonishingly luxurious on the Oklahoma prairie, but the living quarters were still plain.*

RIGHT: *The Lillies' son, Billy, adopted as a baby from an orphan train, died in an accident while playing at the house.*

OPPOSITE: *This upstairs guest room was always saved for Buffalo Bill; note the buffalo skin on the floor. Will Rogers also had a guest room that he regularly used when visiting.*

The guest rooms were all upstairs. Will Rogers slept here. So did Buffalo Bill. Gene Autry and Bob Wills were friends of Pawnee Bill. Rogers regularly used the room overlooking the front lawn; it was comfortable but not lavish, with a slat bed frame and a balcony. Twenty years before Will's own ranch was built, the myth of the West had not yet been codified into steer-horn furniture, wagon-wheel chandeliers, Indian rugs, and rustic log walls. Pawnee Bill's home was less self-conscious about presenting an entire imagined world of the West in design. Buffalo Bill's guest room was only a bit more colorful than Will's; its dark, woolly buffalo hide rug contrasted sharply with the lace curtains.

But this was also the home of a showman. Pawnee Bill had lived the Wild West for a few years, and now he was deeply into the business of turning Indian wars, buffalo hunts, and general derring-do into staged extravaganzas for the entertainment of a public in the Midwest and East that could only dream of such exploits. As an extension of his showmanship, Pawnee Bill's home

showed reality in the process of being transformed into myth. Inset ceramic tile murals over the study and living room fireplaces depicted pioneers and Indians crossing buffalo-filled plains under a brilliant blue sky. Hung over the high wood wainscoting were oil paintings, by Robert Lindneux and others, of Indians and bison and mountains and plains.

Like the home itself, Pawnee Bill's career straddled the eras of the real and mythical frontiers. Lillie had known the end of the real West. As a child in Wellington, Kansas, he had watched the beginning of the end for the Pawnee as they moved from Nebraska to Indian Territory. Once in Oklahoma he had befriended the Pawnee and participated in their annual buffalo hunts. But he was also an active player in the next phase of the West: its mythologizing for profit. As a child he had read dime novels about the fictitious exploits of Buffalo Bill; in 1883 he went to work for his childhood hero as an interpreter for the Pawnee in the Wild West Show. Five years later he started his own show.

Pawnee Bill was an inextricable mix of authentic plainsman and cultivated persona. Near the end of his life in 1939, by then a living legend, he was presented with gold-plated spurs by John Wayne. The symbolism was apt; if it had not been for entertainment, the West would never have survived.

ABOVE: *Gene Autry's picture adorns Pawnee Bill's den. The friendship of the two men shows the overlap of early arena entertainers like Pawnee Bill and Buffalo Bill, who spread the romance of the West, and the later cowboy movie stars who followed in their footsteps.*

OPPOSITE: *After the log cabin's chamber pots, this sparkling, indoor bathroom was one of the prime luxuries of the house.*

ABOVE: *The porch connected the main house to the stone building used as the dining room. The dining room was decked out in tapa cloth and other South Seas decorations the Londons brought back from their journeys.*

OPPOSITE: *London and his wife, Charmian, moved into this ranch house while awaiting the construction of a lavish ranch mansion, Wolf House, nearby. Here he wrote, often in the study he added to the right. He was committed to making his ranch an up-to-date, scientifically based working ranch.*

BEAUTY RANCH: THE JACK LONDON RANCH

GLEN ELLEN, CALIFORNIA, 1911

Jack London's vision of the ranch was that of a radical techno-progressive. While Charles Fletcher Lummis sought a way to express Western life as colonial history and high culture at El Alisal, while Pawnee Bill tried to blend Eastern gentility with prairie lore at Blue Hawk Peak, London looked to modern science to reinvigorate and reinvent the ranch.

London's writing interests may have ranged from socialist politics to sailing the South Seas to prospecting in the Yukon, but when he went home, it was to his native California and his Beauty Ranch in Sonoma County. There he experimented in raising livestock and growing crops by progressive, scientific methods.

London and his wife, Charmian, lived in the simple frame ranch house they had bought on the property of the old K and F Winery in 1911. It had porches front and back; the front ones they enclosed with glass as sleeping porches. By that time London was already building his dream ranch house, Wolf House, nearby. A glorious construction of massive stone foundations and redwood superstructure befitting the world-famous, adventure-loving author, it would have far surpassed Pawnee Bill's ranch house as a wonder in the wilderness.

In the meantime London turned his energies to the Beauty Ranch. He fictionalized his ranching philosophy in *Valley of the Moon*: the protagonists, stand-ins for Jack and Charmian, leave the corrupt city to find a better life in the countryside. They meet immigrant farmers who, through hard work and a willingness to try new techniques, turn depleted farmland to fertile soil. In contrast, old Yankee farmers, unwilling to try new ways in the new century, turn bitter and hateful toward the fresh blood and fresh ideas brought by the immigrants. Change or die seemed to be London's theme.

London applied his scientific approach to the construction of his ranch buildings. A pair of silos were made of newly developed concrete blocks. A piggery was planned in the round, with a tower for storing and mixing feed in the center and a hemicycle of pigpens around it.

The house itself displayed London's wide-ranging knowledge and tastes. With a dining room draped in tapa cloth made from mulberry tree bark and printed with native designs from the South Seas, it may have been the first tiki-style home in California.

Wolf House, which would have been the full embodiment of London's vision, burned days before completion. London never rebuilt. The photogenic and daring adventurer, one of the century's first media stars, had started out to shape the way the nation saw its rural future. But popular culture would turn elsewhere to create its lasting myth of the ranch.

ABOVE: *London experimented enthusiastically with innovative ranching techniques. He invented this circular pig sty; neat pens for each family of pigs ringed the central silo, where feed was stored and mixed.*

OPPOSITE: *London experimented with thoroughbred cattle and horses and tried to raise eucalyptus trees as a cash crop. Today the ranch is a vineyard. The ruined foundations of an old barn are in the foreground.*

ABOVE: *Like many cowboy stars born in the East, silent movie star William S. Hart took on the trappings of the West in his clothing, home, and lifestyle. Situated on a hilltop surrounded by craggy mountains right out of a movie western, the Spanish-style house was part ranch, part Beverly Hills mansion.*

TOP: *Portrait of Hart.*

OPPOSITE: *The exposed wood beams decorated with Native American designs and the Navajo-inspired rugs show this to be a ranch house, while the comfortable furnishings, the paintings, and the grand piano show it to be a glamorized ranch house. Only the wealthy could afford to bestow such careful craftsmanship on such plain elements. The fact that they chose to lavish such care showed that the cowboy style had arrived.*

LA LOMA DE LOS VIENTOS: THE WILLIAM S. HART RANCH

NEWHALL, CALIFORNIA, 1925
ARTHUR KELLEY, ARCHITECT

You could say that Hollywood cowboy star William S. Hart lived above the store.

The silent-movie star known for his two-gun stance, steady stare, and thin lips bought this ranch near the small town of Newhall, outside Los Angeles, in 1921. He had already been using the site for filming his westerns, appropriating its small 1918 wood ranch house as a set; his crew would take off the walls so that they could shoot authentic interiors using natural light.

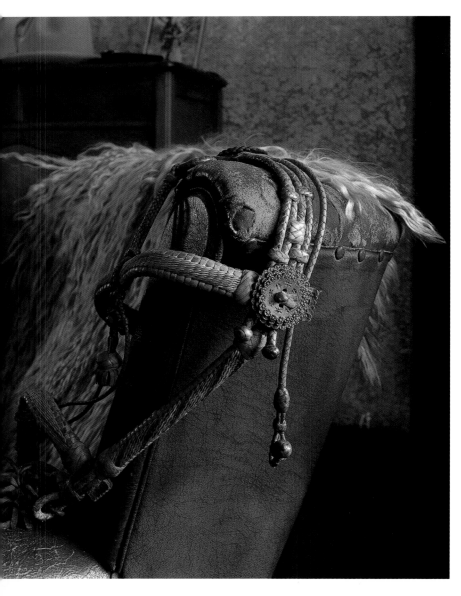

RIGHT: *The back courtyard leads to a tea house and view terrace.*

ABOVE: *A handsome bridle shows both the beauty of genuine handmade fittings and a nostalgia for the romantic image of the Old West that figures in many westerns and in the homes of cowboy stars.*

OPPOSITE: *Portraits of Native Americans circle the entry hall stair; Indian-based patterns can be seen on the ceiling.*

By today's standards, Hart was an unlikely movie star. He had been born in Newburgh, New York. His brush with the real West was working as a cowboy in Kansas; once he was caught in the crossfire between a sheriff and two gunmen. Mostly he had been a stage actor for twenty years before moving to California. He began appearing in films at age 49 with the 1914 production *Two Gun Bill*. His career lasted until *Tumbleweeds* in 1925, after which he retired and began building his home on the hilltop above the movie location.

Like Will Rogers' Pacific Palisades ranch, the Hart house was as much a Beverly Hills home as a ranch. It sat on a hilltop with a commanding view of the Santa Clarita Valley. The landscape itself blurred the line between Western and Hollywood reality; the small country town of Newhall was sometimes used by film crews as a location, and the dramatic mountains around it photographed well in the westerns.

Approached by a winding road, La Loma de los Vientos was an estate with a gatehouse like an Anasazi watchtower, but with friendly red-painted wooden gates that usually stood open. On the grounds Italian cypress stood alongside rustic pines. Like many Beverly Hills homes of the era, the house itself was Spanish in style, though adorned with a bucking-bronco weathervane and wood balconies ornamented in carved and painted wood columns and capitals. The entry was through a rotunda with a spiral stair that led to the grand views from the living room on the second floor. The house was filled with Hart's Western memorabilia, including Navajo blankets, Indian costumes, and Western paintings.

Hart lived almost exactly the same years as Pawnee Bill, whose career as a Wild West show impresario ended the year before Hart's film career began. Together their careers traced the trajectory of the cowboy lifestyle as it passed from living fact to vaudeville entertainment to its celluloid afterlife in the movies. Hart's once-rural house takes the story another step. Today the view that Hart would see from his hilltop—now a county park—embraces the tiled roofs and endless subdivisions of suburbia. Thanks to the movies, the ranch house style lives on in the streets of suburban America.

TOP: *The living room mingles signs of traditional culture such as books and a piano with Western art and Indian artifacts.*

LEFT: *A Conestoga wagon bookend holds up a selection of Western novels.*

OPPOSITE: *One of Hart's trademarks, his tall hat, is now on display at his house, currently a Los Angeles County museum.*

ABOVE: *A portrait of Hart as a steely-eyed cowboy shows some of the character that made him one of the first cowboy movie stars, one who set the standard for everyone who came after him.*

RIGHT: *The heavily textured stucco on the walls of the study was meant to suggest some of the handmade quality of early adobe houses.*

OPPOSITE: *This bedroom combines Craftsman furniture and the simplicity of Spanish adobe.*

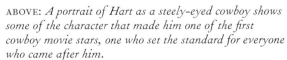

THE WILL ROGERS RANCH

PACIFIC PALISADES, CALIFORNIA, 1928

Will Rogers seems to have been everywhere there was a ranch. He was a friend of Pawnee Bill, he toured California missions with Charles Lummis, he was a guest of Frank Phillips at Woolaroc, he kept polo ponies at Kemper Campbell's Victorville ranch. He also had a ranch of his own, albeit one that was very much a movie star's creation.

The boy from Claremore, Oklahoma, got his start in show business touring with the Miller Brothers' 101 Ranch Show at the turn of the century and ended up as one of Hollywood's highest-paid stars. When he built his last home, he located it off Sunset Boulevard near the Pacific Ocean, far from the prairie.

The Pacific Palisades house was nothing like Rogers' own birthplace in eastern Oklahoma, a simple wood frame building. It echoed the great hotels of Yellowstone and the Grand Canyon. It began in 1928 as a one-story lodge next to the polo field where Rogers rode ponies with friends like Daryl F. Zanuck, Walt Disney, and Hal Roach. The long, rambling wood house has the feel of an oversized, well-to-do suburban home of the 1920s, but one that adopts the rough-hewn luxury of the ranch style. The rustic charms of wood trusses fabricated of peeled logs create an atmosphere of simplicity, no matter how much hard work went into the construction.

ABOVE: *A trellis covered with bougainvillea vines connects the original cabin (left) to the two-story Monterey Colonial addition built when Rogers moved here permanently from Beverly Hills. An outdoor patio with fireplace and mobile barbecue separates the two structures.*

OPPOSITE: *Rogers created a romantic image of a prairie ranch house on an unlikely site near the Pacific Ocean. Part Hollywood stage set, part childhood memory, part homage to Buffalo Bill, the house reflects the casual, unpretentious character of its owner while telling a story about the West. Note the wagon-wheel chandelier, the hanging porch swing, and the carved horse heads supporting wood trusses. The door leads to the kitchen; the stairs lead to guest rooms.*

Over the years Rogers added to the original house. He liked Kemper Campbell's two-story living room with a balcony running along one side, so he raised the roof on his lodge and added a balcony and guest rooms. After he decided to move his wife and three children out of Beverly Hills in 1931, he built a two-story addition, with a dining patio and portable barbecue in between. The flagstone terrace also had an outdoor fireplace for chilly evenings.

The original lodge is a compendium of the cowboy style: stone fireplace, wood paneling, wagon-wheel chandeliers, deer-horn furniture, Morris chairs, Remington and Russell figures, Navajo rugs tossed casually over railings. The family wing, however, is modernized Western. The fireplace andirons are silhouettes of cowboys, but the knotty-pine paneling is stained and polished, lighter in tone than the paneling in the original house. The addition, with its stone base and long second-floor balcony, is less like a cabin and more sophisticated in its Monterey Colonial style.

LEFT: *A bronze polo player on a horse dominates this study desk. The exaggerated rustic wall and door treatment maintains the style of a ranch.*

OPPOSITE: *A stone corner fireplace with built-in bookcase carries out the rustic decor of the house. This area was once used by Rogers' son.*

For all the attention to cowboy detail, for all the stables and corrals, there is no mistaking Rogers' spread for a working ranch. If the polo field in the front yard isn't a dead giveaway, then the four-hole golf course on the front lawn is. This is Hollywood Ranch style, an idealized vision of the outdoors life using an inventive aesthetic of natural materials, self-consciously crude finishes, and recycled elements like wagon-wheel chandeliers—as if that was all they had on hand when they needed lights.

Built twenty years after Pawnee Bill's prairie mansion, this one had no need to import fancy Eastern conventions or classical ornaments. Like Frank Phillips, Rogers could revel in the purity of rough logs bearing the trace of the axe's hacks, of deerskin leather pulled inelegantly over tables, lampshades, and chairs, of antlers stacked up as a table pedestal like amorphous abstract art. The Western aristocracy had found a style they could call their own, and they wore it proudly.

TOP: *The modern kitchen's sink had dual drains.*

RIGHT: *The modern bathroom includes many built-ins but is still a simple and utilitarian space.*

OPPOSITE: *The original cabin was for entertaining, but the addition was strictly for the family. This part of the house mirrored the taste and style of many Hollywood stars of the 1930s.*

ABOVE: *A sombrero and blanket from Tom Mix hang casually from the balcony railing.*

RIGHT: *Rogers' study shows his interest in world travel, his family, the West, and polo.*

OPPOSITE: *This is a kid's cowboy bedroom, for Rogers' younger son. The faux gas lamps and plain walls give the room a bare prairie simplicity, but touches like the wood door rubbed with paint to exaggerate the wood grain show the art in creating the image.*

ABOVE: *A circular horse ring forms the center of the stable.*

LEFT: *The estate included stalls for Rogers' polo ponies and riding horses.*

BELOW: *Clustered around the stables of the ranch are corrals, riding rings, polo fields, and a special cage to allow Rogers to practice his polo swing.*

OPPOSITE: *A favorite saddle and an Indian drum are displayed in the living room along with many other gifts and artifacts Rogers gathered as a movie star.*

ABOVE: *The McCrea family on the front porch in 1940: left to right, David, Frances Dee, Joel, and Jody.*

OPPOSITE: *Nestled on a hillside, the McCrea ranch was both family home and working ranch. A wood frame board-and-batten structure typical of historic ranch houses, it rambles casually over the sloping site.*

THE JOEL MCCREA RANCH

THOUSAND OAKS, CALIFORNIA, 1933

For all the drugstore cowboys in Hollywood, it's surprising to realize that there were real cowboys in Tinseltown, too. Joel McCrea was one of them.

McCrea's 2,300-acre ranch in Thousand Oaks—far out in the country in 1933—was unlike Will Rogers' polo ranch, or Hopalong Cassidy's splendid hilltop spread, or Gene Autry's Studio City estate. McCrea's was a working ranch as well as a home. He and his wife raised three children there. After a day at the studio he would come home to tend the ranch, brand the calves, mend the fences. It was not a large operation; he had one or two men working for him, plus his sons when they were old enough. His day job in the movies made the ranch possible, but it was a real ranch nonetheless.

McCrea, the star of many westerns as well as other kinds of movies, came by the cowboy heritage honestly. He grew up in Los Angeles when it was a major ranching and agricultural region as well as the mecca of world cinema. There were plenty of ranches just over the hill from Hollywood in the San Fernando Valley. As a young man McCrea drove horses for a job. Like thousands of others, he decided to get work as an extra in westerns. Unlike thousands of others, he was noticed.

ABOVE: *Brick and wood sections of the house show the character of the ranch house, adapting and growing with time.*

OPPOSITE: *The simple wood post structure and board siding of this custom ranch house became popular features of suburban tract ranch houses after World War II.*

While appearing in *Lightning* in 1929, McCrea was befriended by the film's star, the ubiquitous Will Rogers. They were both cowboys, after all. Rogers helped him get his start in the movies and provided the model for investing in a ranch. McCrea chose the ranch in Thousand Oaks soon after.

McCrea's ranch became part of the shadow Hollywood West, a real West of working ranches and weekend rodeos. Its inhabitants often had day jobs as actors, stunt men, wranglers, or operators of the movie ranches. A movie ranch was one where westerns were filmed; examples included Corriganville, the Iverson Ranch, the Paramount Ranch, Gene Autry's Melody Ranch, the Ingram Ranch, and the Jauregui Ranch. In the photogenic and varied scenery around Los Angeles, the rock spires, box canyons, and rolling prairies of the movie West could all be found. These ranches also had false-front towns and ranch houses. Sometimes they were one-time working ranches rented out to studios; sometimes they were newly constructed as sets.

The movie ranches were yet another step in blurring the lines between the real West and the West of Hollywood. Many working ranches like the San Rafael in Arizona have been used in westerns; here, Hollywood sets were used for rodeos and sometimes were populated by real cowboys like Joel McCrea. In the interplay of the genuine West and its re-creation in the movies, it is not always easy to distinguish cleanly between what is real and what is fake, what is authentic and what is a representation, what is reality and what is myth. Was Buffalo Bill an actor or a Pony Express rider? But it is fitting to note that McCrea's sons, raised in this ambiguous world of the Hollywood West, became full-time ranchers themselves.

ABOVE: *Far enough away from Hollywood and the studios, movie star Joel McCrea and his wife could raise their family in a real ranch setting.*

OPPOSITE: *The mud porch was a useful way to keep dirt out of the ranch house.*

THE HOPALONG CASSIDY RANCH

MALIBU, CALIFORNIA, 1934

William Boyd's ranch house was as much a part of his Hopalong Cassidy costume as his black outfit and matching hat. It was, in effect, an architectural costume. Its Spanish stucco ornamented with blooming geraniums, its sociable living room with a walk-in fireplace, and its handcrafted doors and beams conveyed a life of rural splendor and generous conviviality. This hilltop palace symbolized the way a cowboy star ought to live, on top of the world, in sunshine and moonlight, between a classically rugged mountain ridge right out of the movies on one side and the blue Pacific on the other. Glorying in its rustic handcrafts, Spanish heritage, and Indian artifacts, the ranch is straight off the page of a movie fan magazine.

"A mini-San Simeon," Boyd's wife, Grace, calls it. It does have the same air of splendid isolation as Hearst's domain farther up the California coast. But the Boyd house is more personal, a real home where friends could visit and not feel they were attending a convention.

Now the site of the Lazy J children's camp, the hilltop home remains in beautiful condition. Remarkably, it still contains many of Hopalong's original furnishings even though he and Grace moved away in 1942. He had built it in 1934, with wagons bringing the materials up the steep canyon's dirt road from the Pacific Coast

ABOVE: *Hopalong Cassidy, originally a literary character, was made famous by William Boyd's movie portrayal.*

OPPOSITE: *Grace Boyd called the hilltop home "a miniature San Simeon." The size of the living room—and its walk-in fireplace—do recall W. R. Hearst's mansion farther up California's coast. Sixty-five feet long, the living room is spanned by solid wood timbers rubbed with paint to emphasize the hand-adzed texture.*

ABOVE: *The Spanish-style ranch takes historic ranchos as a starting point and imaginatively elaborates on them, like a good story, to create an atmosphere in which a romaniticized version of the Old West comes alive.*

OPPOSITE: *Thick wood logs, brought by wagon up the steep hill to the ranch, span the large living room. Here Grace and William Boyd entertained Hollywood friends, often with a fire roaring in the ten-foot-wide fireplace. The windows look out to the Pacific Ocean.*

Highway. When he and Grace were married three years later, she brought her own touch to the house, lining the winding drive with pots of geraniums, landscaping the grounds, adding flower beds.

Everything about the house is self-consciously Western. The plaster walls are finished in a wavy, uneven ripple, as if the rustic craftsman lacked the skill to finish it off by smooth Eastern standards—and didn't much care. The doors of the bedroom wing are a remarkable ornament: the solid wood planks are worked with a hand adze to create a criss-cross pattern with a relief your hand can feel running across it. Each of the foot-thick beams spanning the huge living room is also hand finished and rubbed with stain to bring out the uneven texture. The room itself is some sixty-five feet long.

Any cowboy's best friend is his horse, and Hopalong treated Topper (and his wife's horse, Turnaround) with proper respect. Down the hill from the house he built a small corral and a stone tower for the horses. A big stone water trough remains.

The ranch was so successful as part of a western star's persona that it served as the home of a second movie cowboy as well. Duncan Renaldo, who played the Cisco Kid, lived in the house in the 1960s.

ABOVE: *The study features wood ceilings, ocean views, and an arched fireplace inglenook as well as horse trophies.*

TOP: *The master bathroom features an explosion of colorful tiles.*

RIGHT: *Tall ceilings dominate the bedrooms. Each door is handmade, down to the pattern left by woodworking tools in the grain.*

OPPOSITE: *The master bedroom's sun corner includes many of the original furnishings.*

LEFT: *The current owners of the Hopalong Cassidy Ranch carry on the Boyds' love of horses, as seen on the hallway walls. The living room is to the right, the master bedroom to the left.*

ABOVE: *Kitchen shutters fold against the sides of a thick window frame.*

OPPOSITE: *The country kitchen has Spanish tiles backing the stovetop. The oven and rotisserie (right) are original to the house.*

TODAY'S COWBOYS

THROUGH movies, song, and real estate developments, the ranch house lives on. Contemporary ranch-style homes show the influence of Hollywood's West as much as that of the humble prairie homes seen in Chapter 1.

LEFT: *Craggy stone spires of the classic Hollywood Western landscape march right into the living room of this latter-day ranch.*

ABOVE: *The classic ranch board-and-batten walls echo the vertical pinnacles in the distance.*

OPPOSITE: *Rather than re-creating a movie ranch house, the house borrows the false-front architecture of a Western town familiar to the public from a thousand westerns.*

HAUER RANCH

MOAB, UTAH, 1992
DICK KNECHT, ARCHITECT

At the end of the trail, the ranch house, which began as a simple shelter for cowboys working the range, has become an icon of a way of life. How it got there has been a long story. But it is clear that the movies took a simple vernacular architecture, imbued it with a character far beyond its original intent, and then etched that icon permanently into the popular imagination.

The Hauer Ranch is filled with moments and shapes, views and details that come straight out of the movies' vision of the ranch. Although used as a home, it looks like the false-front set of a town built for a movie western. The main house is two stories, with an Italianate molding along its top; the one-story assay office set at a right angle nearby is the guest house. Whether this is a town or a movie set of a town is completely ambiguous. In fact, several movies, including *The Comancheros*, *Rio Grande*, and *Wagonmaster*, were filmed in the immediate area; a glance out the front door at the distant vista of red buttes and crumbling mesas triggers memories of dozens of films. But the house was never a movie set; it was built long after the movie crews left. It honors both the movies and the ranches.

Inside, the house plays with the image of the ranch. The two-story living room is built against one wall of natural rock; a glass window fills in the jagged gap between two of the great boulders. The rocks seem to be taking over the familiar scene of peeled logs and pine paneling. The interior is configured like a barroom in a movie western. The encircling balcony is where, in the movies, a fistfight would send one combatant head over heels onto a poker table while the ladies of the bordello upstairs draped themselves over the railing to watch. The surreal clash of this textbook cinematic image and the massive force of the stones, frozen as they crash through the scene, is a vivid statement of how the ranch image has altered over the years. Forces beyond its control, this time nature, are once again overtaking the Wild West. The ante has been upped. At Woolaroc the crude, hand-hewn beams of raw timber sneered at the refinements of civilization and Classical style; now nature itself is forcing its presence into the human habitation.

TOP: *The warm glow of light flickers amid the rocks like a campfire at dusk.*

RIGHT: *Here the historic ranch house literally blends into the rocky landscape. A gap between boulders is enclosed with glass.*

OPPOSITE: *The ranch house turns into one of humankind's earliest housing types, the cave.*

This house is richly symbolic of twentieth-century architecture's interaction with the movies. The images from the westerns are all there, but they are put together in striking and unexpected ways. Earlier, Will Rogers helped to codify the cowboy style by bringing together the Western paraphernalia of lariats, wagon wheels, steer horns, saddles, and Navajo rugs into a complete and cohesive statement of the ranch as American metaphor. Now, late in the century, the Hauer Ranch takes the development of the ranch house a step further. It collects the paraphernalia of the cowboy movies themselves. It uses the celluloid image of the West as its source—a perfectly reasonable thing to do in a century when the movies have done so much to shape the popular imagination.

In the beginning, the movies were fascinated by the utilitarian ranch house. They took it over and made it their own, reshaping and intensifying the new Western aesthetic as they went along. At the end of the century, we have come full circle to a ranch house thoroughly shaped by the movies.

TOP: *Knotty-pine paneling and wood trusses carry the rustic ranch exterior indoors.*

LEFT: *As at Will Rogers' ranch, the everyday necessities of historic ranches are turned into ornament and style in latter-day ranch houses. Here a rope, rifle, and knife become decorative objects.*

OPPOSITE: *A cluster of antlers creates a chandelier over one of the bedrooms.*

ABOVE: *The ranch also includes a historic log cabin.*

RIGHT: *With distant buttes framed by wood columns, every view from the Hauer Ranch is a frame from a John Ford movie.*

OPPOSITE: *The natural wall of a boulder forms one wall of the ranch house.*

ACKNOWLEDGMENTS

○   ○   ○

SO MANY PEOPLE made our travels through the land-scape and the history of the West in the course of writing and photographing this book enjoyable, pleas-urable, and satisfying. We want to extend our gratitude and appreciation to all; we were reminded again and again that hospitality, friendliness, and generosity are time-honored qualities of Westerners.

In particular we thank the owners of the ranches who allowed us to visit, and who shared their knowledge and their love for their homesteads. Their devotion has allowed these places to survive into the twenty-first century—a tremendous contribution to the culture and architecture of America. Our thanks to Sarah Bailey, Ninia Bivins, Robert and Murnie Cox, Jean DeBlasis, Frederick Drummond, James Guercio, John and Nancy Hauer, Lucia Howard, Geri Johnson, Margaret Majua, the McCrea family, Katsy Mullendore Mecom, Jean Neubauer, Penny Pollock, Richard Reicheg, Gretchen Sammis, and David Weingarten.

Equally important are the museums, colleges, and state parks that help to preserve these ranches for future generations. We were helped by staff members who treat these ranches as if they were their own. Our thanks to Harvey Payne and the Nature Conservancy; Susan Alvarez and Roger McLendon of the Hearst Hacienda; Ellen Calomiris and the Rancho Los Cerritos Association; Lilla Jones and Jim Pfluger of the Ranching Heritage Center; Linda Stone and Woolaroc; Wanda Green and Randy Ledford at Pawnee Bill State Park; Greg Hayes and Jack London State Park; the Los Angeles County Museum of Natural History; the Lummis House Foundation; Earlyn Mosher and Soka University; Peter DeLuca and St. Thomas Aquinas College; Anne Reinders and the Ventura County Museum of History and Art; Michael Allan and Will Rogers State Park; Taraneh Rohani and the Fountain Valley School; and the Yorba Linda Historical Society.

Then there are the friends and acquaintances who provided information, support, leads, ideas, and encour-agement. Our great thanks go to Noureen Baer, Grace Boyd, Sheila Bricher-Wade and Wyoming's State Office of Historic Preservation, David Bricker, Susan and Larry Cobb, Linda and Jay Colliatie, Carol Doherty, Bill Ehrheart, Marva Felchlin of the Gene Autry Museum of Western Heritage, Nancy Fox, Dale and Shirley Furman, Pixie Geren, Sean Gilbert, Karen Glasser, Ruby Gobble, Daniel Gregory, Virginia Hall, Maxine Hansen of Gene Autry Entertainment, Jack Harding, Curt Helfrich and the University of California, Santa Barbara, Drawing Collections, Debbie and Todd Herzer, Charles Hess, Deborah and Herb Huebsch, Alan Jutzi of the Huntington Library, Dick Knecht, David McCrea, Wyatt McCrea, Wallace Neff, Jr., Lynn Pitet and the McCracken Research Library of the Buffalo Bill Historical Center, Cheryl Rogers-Barnett and the Roy Rogers-Dale Evans Museum, Jerry Rosenthal, Tom Starkweather, Eric Stevens, Nash and Zoe Stone-Hess, Laura and Joe Warriner, Edson Way, and Marie Wootten. Special appreciation goes to our friends at Chronicle Books, Nion McEvoy and Christina Wilson, for their patience and support. And, as always, the inspiration of John Beach and David Gebhard led the way to a new appreciation of Western architecture.

If we have inadvertently left anyone out, we regret the omission deeply. This book would not have been possible without the help of all of you.

BIBLIOGRAPHY

○ ○ ○

Alexander, Drury B. *Texas Homes of the Nineteenth Century*. Austin: University of Texas Press, 1966.

Apostol, Jan. *El Alisal: Where History Lingers*. Los Angeles: Historical Society of Southern California, 1994.

Armstrong, Ruth W. *The Chases of Cimarron: Birth of the Cattle Industry in Cimarron Country, 1867-1900*. Albuquerque: New Mexico Stockman, 1981.

Autry, Gene. *Back in the Saddle Again*. New York: Doubleday, 1978.

Clayton, Lawrence. *Historic Ranches of Texas*. Austin: University of Texas Press, 1993.

Dary, David. *Cowboy Culture: A Saga of Five Centuries*. New York: Knopf, 1981.

Georgen, Cynde. *One Cowboy's Dream: John B. Kendrick—His Family, Home and Ranching Empire*. Sheridan, Wyoming: Trail End Guilds, 1995.

Johnson, Paul C., ed. *Western Ranch Houses by Cliff May*. Santa Monica, California: Hennessey + Ingalls, 1997.

Reeve, Agnesa Lufkin. *From Hacienda to Bungalow: Northern New Mexico Houses, 1850-1912*. Albuquerque: University of New Mexico Press, 1988.

Rosa, Joseph G., and Robin May. *Buffalo Bill and His Wild West*. Lawrence: University Press of Kansas, 1989.

Rothel, Davi. *The Roy Rogers Book*. Madison, North Carolina: Empire Publishing, 1987.

Russell, Don. *The Lives and Legends of Buffalo Bill*. Norman: University of Oklahoma Press, 1960.

Starr, Eileen F. *Architecture in the Cowboy State, 1849-1940*. Glendo, Wyoming: High Plains Press, 1992.

Stewart, Janet Ann. *Arizona Ranch Houses: Southern Territorial Style, 1867-1900*. Phoenix: Arizona Historical Society, 1974.

Stoechlein, David. *Texas Cowboys*. Ketchum, Idaho: Stoechlin Publishing, 1996.

Wallis, Michael. *Oil Man: The Story of Frank Phillips and the Birth of Phillips Petroleum*. New York: Doubleday, 1988.

Wayne, Pilar. *John Wayne: My Life with the Duke*. New York: McGraw-Hill, 1977.

PAGE 202: *The Hauer Ranch*.

LEFT: *Woolaroc, the Frank Phillips Ranch*.

INDEX

ALAN HESS is the author of *Googie* and *Viva Las Vegas*, both published by Chronicle Books. He lives in San Francisco.

ALAN WEINTRAUB is a San Francisco–based photographer whose work appears in architectural and design publications throughout the world. His books include *San Francisco Interiors*, *California Cottages*, and *California Wine Country*, all published by Chronicle Books.